I0759629

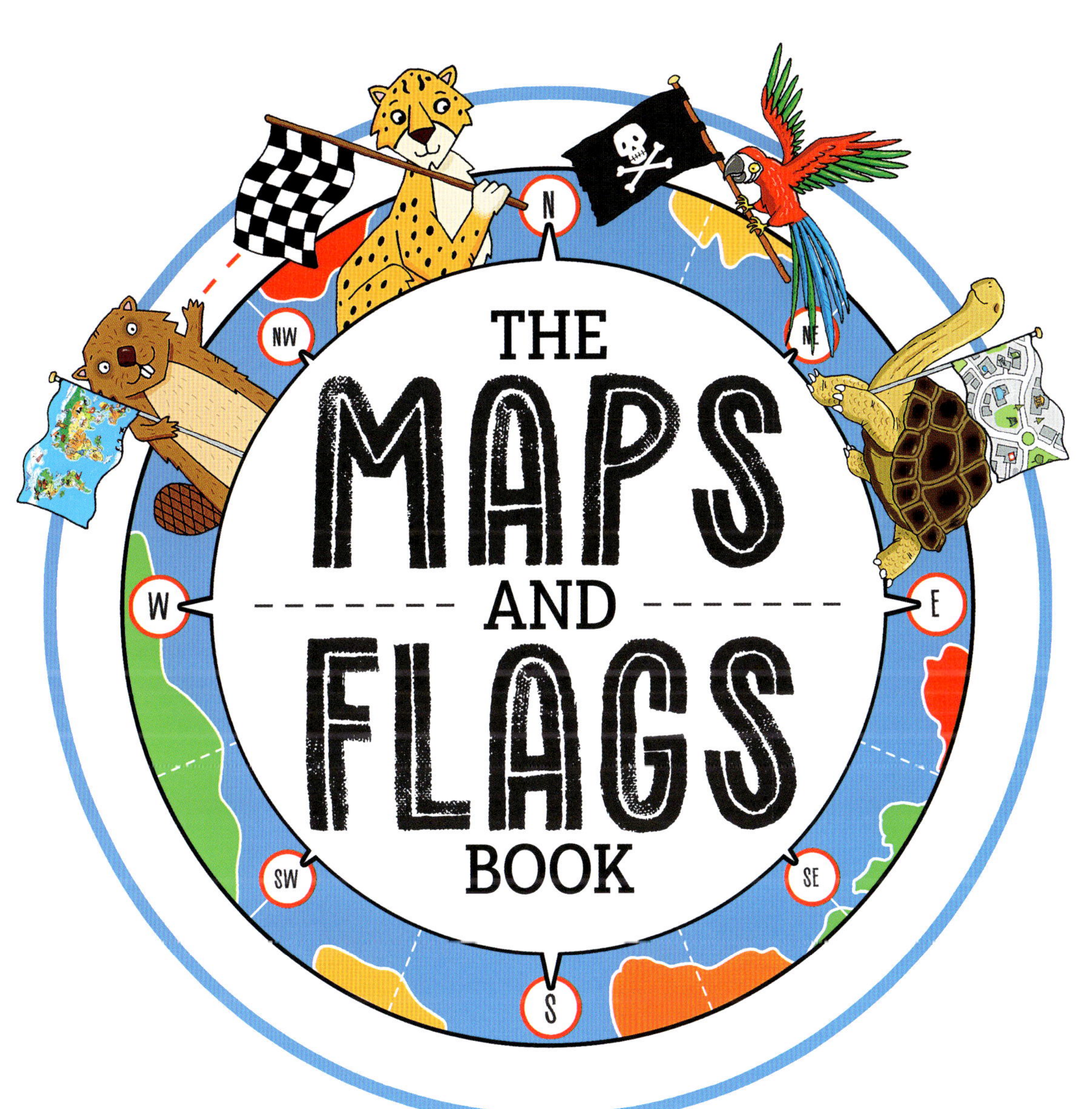
THE
MAPS
AND
FLAGS
BOOK
N
NE
E
SE
S
SW
W
NW

PROJECT MANAGED BY JAM BOOKS

WRITTEN BY JOE FULLMAN
ILLUSTRATED BY ANDY ROWLAND
EDITED BY EMMA TAYLOR
DESIGNED BY ANDY MANSFIELD
COVER DESIGN BY ANGIE ALLISON

Manufacturer: First published in Great Britain in 2025 by Buster Books, an imprint of Michael O'Mara Books Limited, 9 Lion Yard, Tremadoc Road, London SW4 7NQ
www.mombooks.com

Represented by: Authorised Rep Compliance Ltd, Ground Floor, 71 Lower Baggot Street, Dublin D02 P593, Ireland
www.arccompliance.com

 www.mombooks.com/buster  Buster Books  @buster_books

A CIP catalogue record for this book is available from the British Library.

ISBN: 978-1-83725-096-7

3 5 7 9 10 8 6 4 2

This product is made of material from well-managed, FSC®-certified forests and other controlled sources. The manufacturing processes conform to the environmental regulations of the country of origin.

Printed and bound in December 2025 by
Oriental Press, Street Number N605, Roundabout 5,
Jebel Ali Free Zone 22008, Dubai, UAE.

For further information see www.mombooks.com/about/sustainability-climate-focus
Report any safety issues to product.safety@mombooks.com

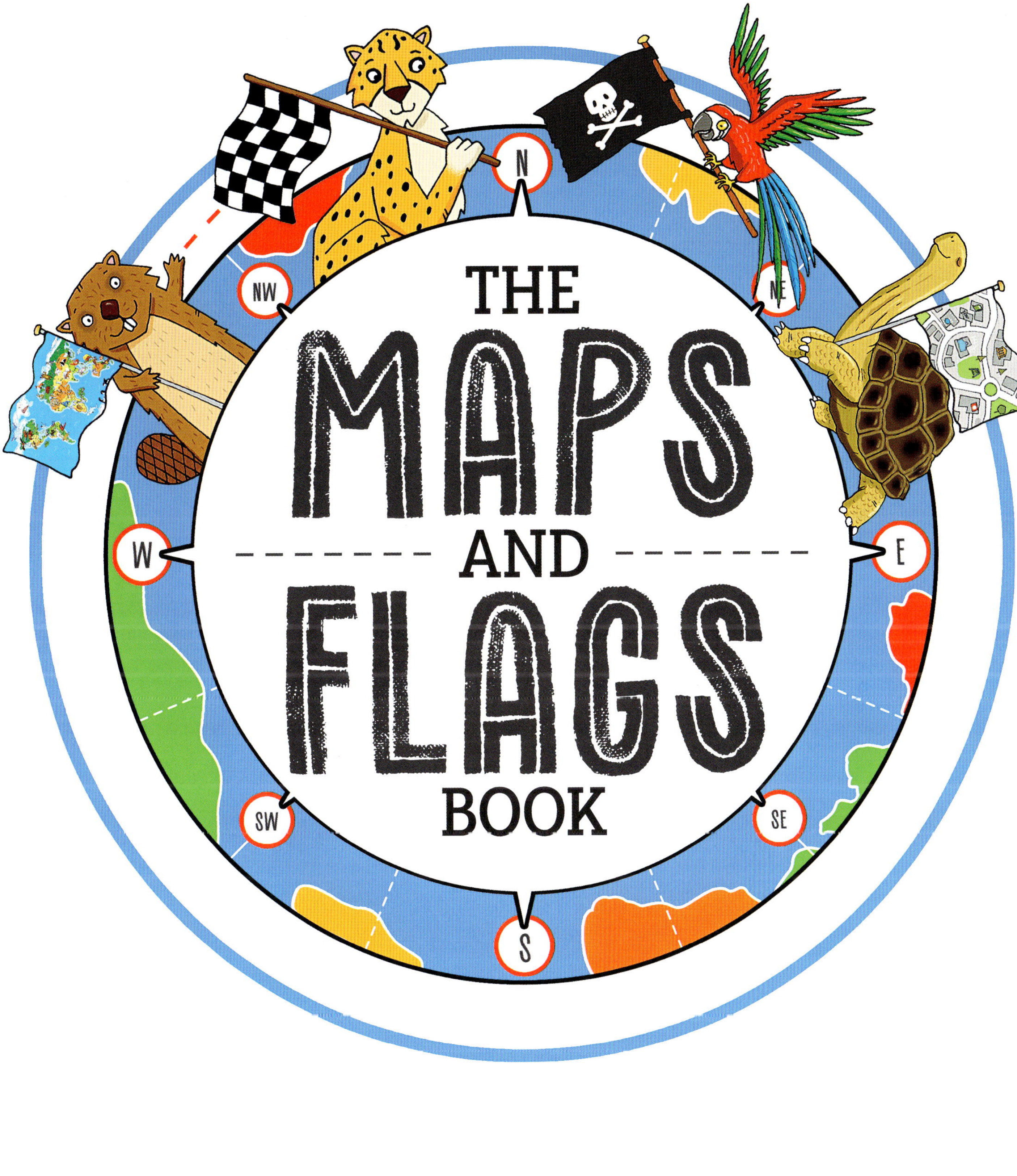

THE MAPS AND FLAGS BOOK

BUSTER BOOKS

CONTENTS

INTRODUCTION

This book takes a close-up look at maps and flags, two of the most important ways to visually represent a country. A map shows the shape of a country's land and where its major cities and other features are located. A flag provides a colorful, recognizable image of a country to be displayed around the world. Studying maps and flags can provide a fascinating insight into the differences—and similarities—between countries.

Animal characters such as me will be popping up throughout this book to tell you a bit more about the maps and flags of our areas.

WHAT IS A COUNTRY?

In this book, we show the flag and a simple map of every country on Earth. But what exactly is a country? It can be a surprisingly difficult thing to describe, as there's no internationally recognized definition. But, in general terms, it should be possible to say all the things in this list about a country:

- **It should be an area of land with clearly defined borders that can be shown on a map.**
- **It should have people living there permanently.**
- **It should have a government that represents the people to other countries.**
- **It (and its flag) should be recognized as a country by a majority of other countries.**

This map shows the mainland of the United States of America (USA). **Turn to p.16 to find out more.**

OVERSEAS TERRITORIES

Not every area of land on Earth is a country. Some areas of land belong to other countries and are often known as overseas territories. See p.92 for more about these areas.

Most countries are members of the United Nations, an international organization where countries come together to discuss and debate world issues. It also has its own flag, which I'm waving here.

HOW THIS BOOK WORKS

This book is divided into regions, made up of the five continents of North America, South America, Europe, Africa, and Asia, plus the continental region of Oceania (which includes the continent of Australia).

WORLD AND CONTINENT MAPS

There's a map of the world on pages 12–13, showing the location of the continents. Each chapter also starts with a map of the continent or region being featured, such as this one for South America (see p.25). This illustrates where all the continent's countries are located, alongside some additional information and fun facts.

MONTENEGRO

FLAG

POPULATION: 600,000
AREA: 13,812 sq km
CURRENCY: Euro
FLAG ADOPTED: 2004

STATS

COUNTRY MAP

Podgorica

FLAG FACT: Montenegro's flag is based on a historic royal banner, and features the coat of arms of a dynasty who once ruled the country.

FLAG FACT

COUNTRY FLAGS AND MAPS

Each country gets its own section, such as this one for Montenegro in Europe (see p.45). In it, you'll see the country's flag as well as a simple map of the country's borders and the location of its capital city. Extra stats about the country's population, area, and currency are also provided, along with a fact giving background information on the country's flag.

MORE MAPS

There are many kinds of maps—weather maps, wildlife maps, pirate maps, and more. These are explored in the "More About Maps" feature at the end of each chapter. Here, you'll see examples of some of the different types of maps, such as these transportation maps at the end of the Europe chapter (see p.48).

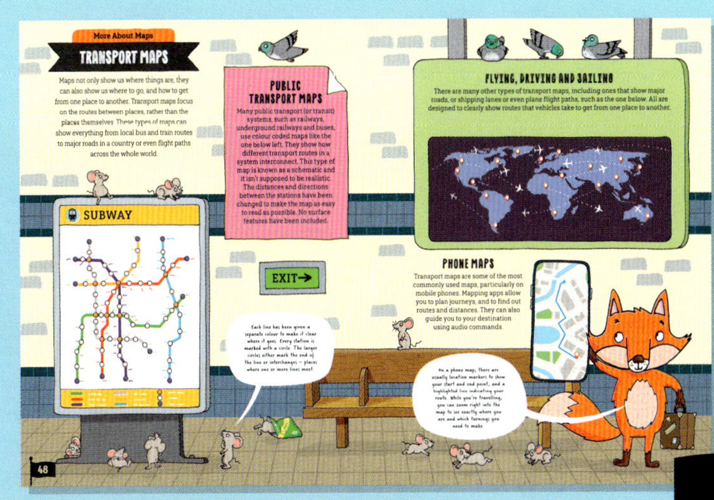

WHAT IS A MAP?

A map is a picture of an area as if seen from above. There are many types of maps, which can be used to display lots of different kinds of information, but all work in much the same way. They use colors and symbols to represent an area's shape and features.

MAPS OF BIG AREAS

In order to show somewhere on a map, all the features of that area need to be shrunk down by the same amount. This is known as the scale. Some maps, such as this map of the world, show a very large area, but they can't show a lot of detail.

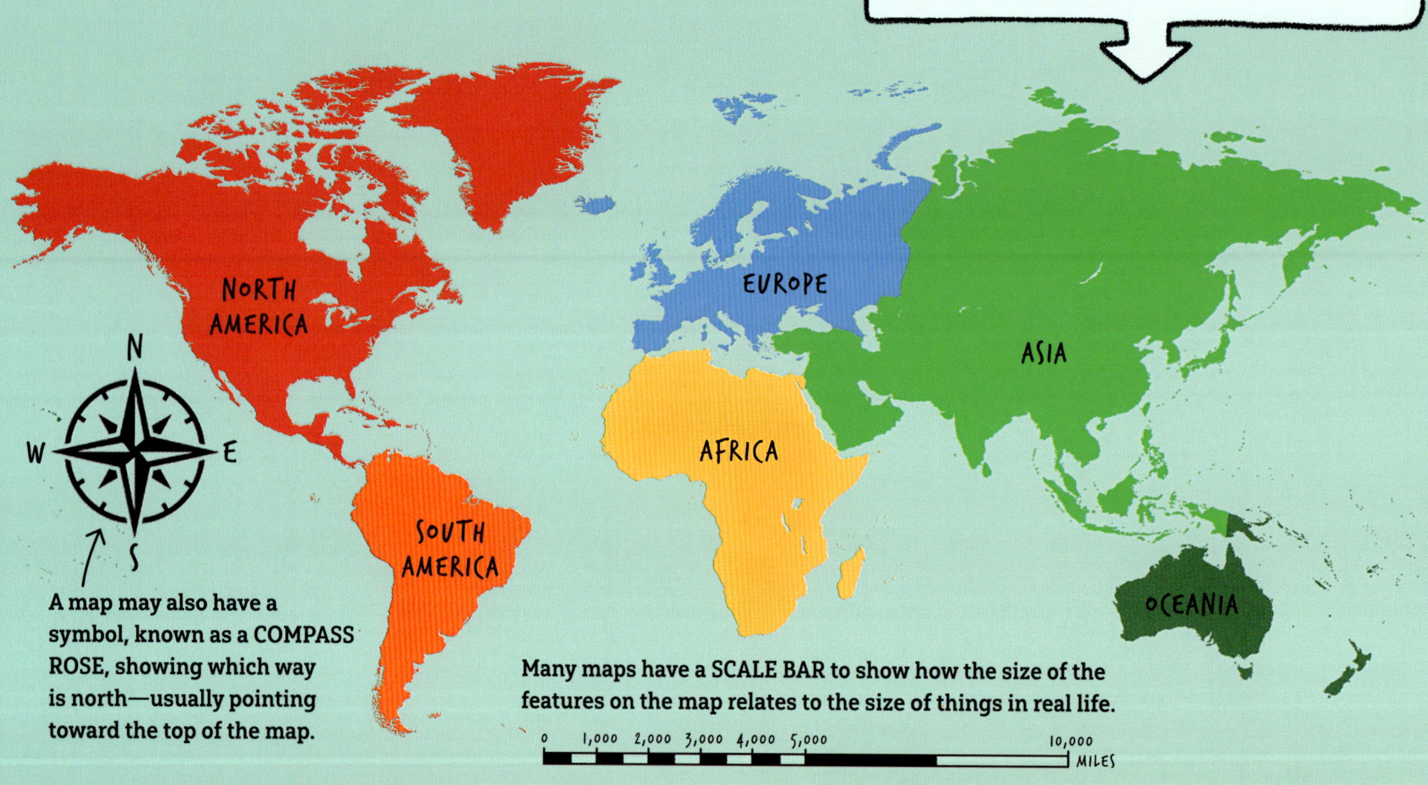

A map may also have a symbol, known as a COMPASS ROSE, showing which way is north—usually pointing toward the top of the map.

Many maps have a SCALE BAR to show how the size of the features on the map relates to the size of things in real life.

0 1,000 2,000 3,000 4,000 5,000 10,000 MILES

MAPS OF SMALL AREAS

Maps can also show very small areas, such as a town or even a few streets. These types of maps can show a lot of detail.

SYMBOLS

Symbols are small pictures that represent a particular feature or type of place on a map. The meaning of each symbol is explained in the map's key. Colors can also be used to highlight certain areas, such as parks (in green) or rivers (in blue).

KEY

PARKING LOT

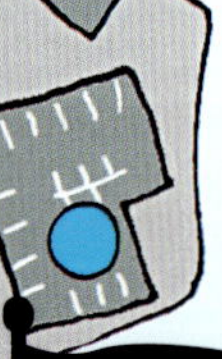

POLITICAL MAPS

Most of the maps in this book are political maps. These show how an area of land is divided into countries or states. This means the maps display some features that you can't actually see on the ground, such as borders—the lines that divide one country from another. Political maps often use colors to highlight the different shapes of the countries.

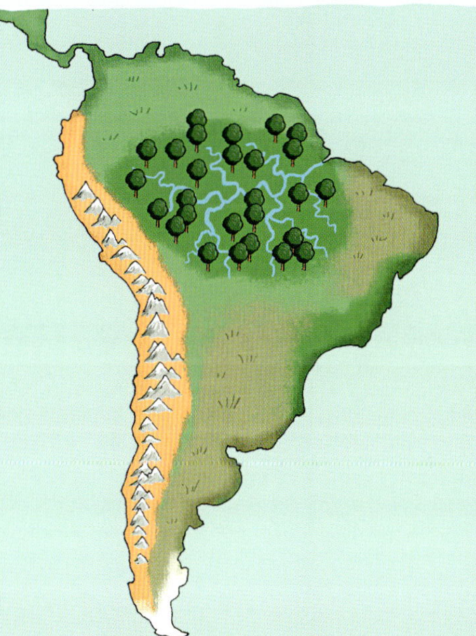

PHYSICAL MAPS

A physical map shows the natural features of a landscape, such as mountains, valleys, and rivers. It may also use colors to show different habitats, such as green for forests, gray for mountains, and orange for deserts. Shading can also be used to indicate areas of higher and lower ground.

THEMATIC MAPS

Some maps focus on a particular topic or theme. They may show what the weather is like in an area, the main transportation routes in a city, or where animals live in a continent. Maps are a great way of showing the answers to simple questions, such as "Which countries drive on the left, and which drive on the right?" or "What are the favorite foods of countries around the world?"

WHAT IS A FLAG?

A flag is a visual symbol designed to represent something, such as a country or an institution. It usually takes the form of a rectangular piece of material decorated with a colorful design, which is held up by a flagpole. Every country in the world has a flag with its own unique pattern. Many regions, states, and cities also have their own flags.

PARTS OF A FLAG

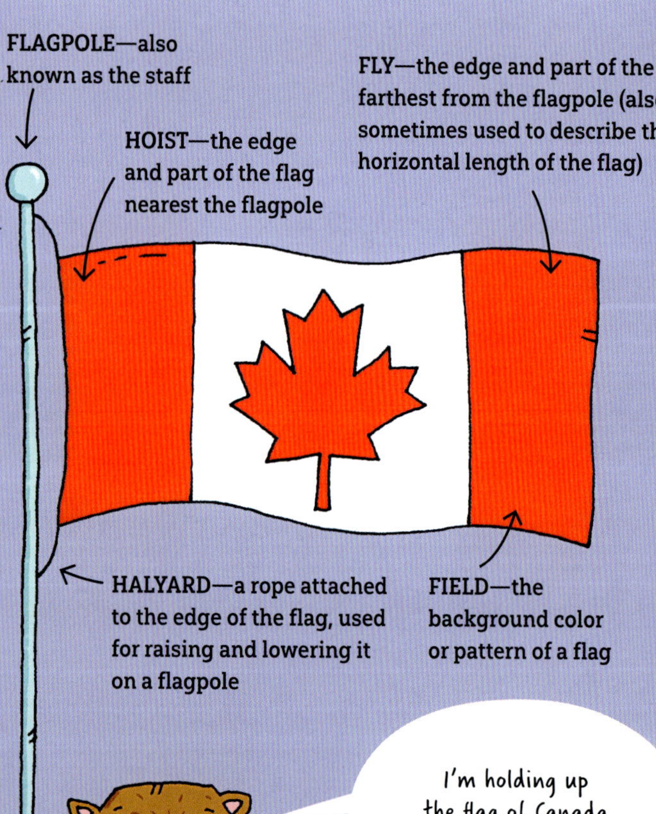

I'm holding up the flag of Canada (p.16). At its center is a picture of one of the country's most important symbols, the maple leaf. It's almost as important as the national animal, the beaver.

FLAG SHAPES

The majority of country flags are rectangular. Switzerland and the Vatican City (p.43) have square flags, while Nepal is the only country to have a five-sided flag known as a double pennant.

FLAG OF SWITZERLAND (p.40)

FLAG OF NEPAL (p.76)

RATIOS

Flags often have different ratios—the contrast between their height and their width. The flag of Switzerland is square, giving it a ratio of 1:1. The flag of France has a ratio of 2:3, which means it is one and a half times as long as it is wide. The UK flag has a ratio of 1:2, making it twice as long as it is wide.

FLAG OF FRANCE, 2:3 (p.41)

FLAG OF THE UNITED KINGDOM, 1:2 (p.37)

FLAG PATTERNS

Each flag has its own distinctive design to make it easily recognizable, but there are certain patterns that are common to many flags.

CANTON: a rectangular section in the top left where a design (or another flag) is displayed —e.g., Australia (p.89)

CHARGE: a symbol, such as a plant, an animal, a religious symbol, or a mythical creature —e.g., Albania (p.46)

CHEVRON: a triangle or V-shape, usually shown coming in from the side of the flag —e.g., The Bahamas (p.18)

COAT OF ARMS: a design made up of symbols and mottos that represent the country —e.g., Ecuador (p.26)

CROSS, SYMMETRICAL: made by vertical and horizontal lines intersecting at the flag's center, —e.g., Georgia (p.70)

CROSS, OFF-CENTER: made by vertical and horizontal lines intersecting on one side —e.g., Sweden (p.34)

CROSS, DIAGONAL: made by diagonal lines intersecting at the center of the flag —e.g., Jamaica (p.19)

FESSES: horizontal bands or stripes running across the width of the flag —e.g., Lithuania (p.35)

PALES: vertical bands or stripes on a flag, often in groups of three —e.g., Côte d'Ivoire (p.56)

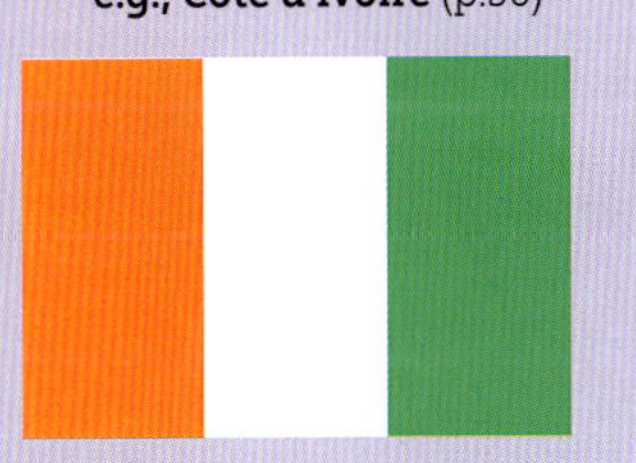

FLYING FLAGS

It's not just countries that fly flags. Areas within countries, such as states and provinces, often have their own flags, as do some presidents and royal families. Ships fly flags to show which country they are registered with, and there are even sports that use flags, such as auto racing.

A checkered flag is waved to tell drivers that the race is over.

THE WORLD'S CONTINENTS

The world is made up of seven continents. Most of the world's people live in six of these: North America, South America, Europe, Africa, Asia, and Australia. The seventh continent, Antarctica, right at the southern end of the world, is too cold and inhospitable for people to stay there permanently. In this book, we'll travel around the world to each of the continents in turn, to look at the maps and flags of the countries and territories there.

PACIFIC OCEAN

NORTH AMERICA

ATLANTIC OCEAN

SOUTH AMERICA

FROM GLOBE TO MAP

Earth is shaped like a ball, and so the most accurate map of the planet is a globe. To get the areas of land on a curved globe to fit onto a flat map, mapmakers have to distort, or change, the shape of the areas slightly. This is known as making a projection.

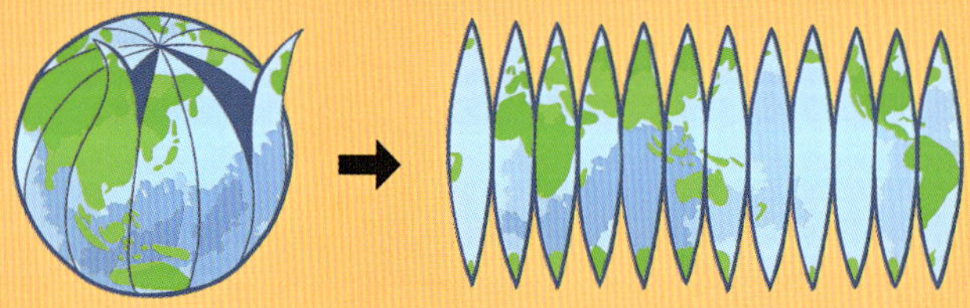

Imagine peeling a globe like an orange, and then trying to press the pieces of peel down flat. There will be gaps in between them. Mapmakers have to tweak the shapes of the land to get them to match up across the gaps.

North America and South America used to be completely separate. They are now linked by a narrow strip of land known as the Isthmus of Panama, which formed around 3 million years ago.

WHAT IS A CONTINENT?

A continent is very large landmass that is mostly separated from any other very large landmass. There may be a small piece of land linking two continents, as is the case with North and South America. Europe and Asia really form one big landmass, which is sometimes referred to as a single continent: Eurasia.

Europe and Asia have been regarded as separate continents since ancient times. The division was based more on culture and history than geography. Many animals, such as us gray wolves, live in both.

ARCTIC OCEAN

EUROPE

ASIA

Home to around 4.6 billion people, Asia is the most-populated continent.

PACIFIC OCEAN

AFRICA

INDIAN OCEAN

Australia lies within a larger continental region called Oceania, which also includes New Zealand and many smaller islands.

AUSTRALIA

THE OCEANS

Land makes up only 29 percent of Earth's surface. The other 71 percent is water. Although it forms an unbroken body of water across the planet, we divide it into five oceans: the Arctic, the Pacific, the Atlantic, the Indian, and the Southern Oceans.

There are around 40 million of us penguins living in Antarctica, but only about 5,000 people. Most are visiting scientists working at research stations.

SOUTHERN OCEAN

ANTARCTICA

NORTH AMERICA

Stretching from close to the North Pole down to the tropics, this vast territory is dominated by three big countries: Canada, the USA, and Mexico. But there are plenty of smaller ones, too, in Central America and the Caribbean. Habitats range from the evergreen forests of the north, where wolves and bears prowl, to the great plains of the center, the deserts of the southwest, and the lush rainforests of the south.

NORTH AMERICA FACTS

- **SIZE:** 9.6 million sq mi (25 million sq km)
- **NO. OF COUNTRIES:** 23
- **POPULATION:** 596 million
- **LARGEST COUNTRY BY AREA:** Canada
- **LARGEST COUNTRY BY POPULATION:** USA
- **SMALLEST COUNTRY BY AREA AND POPULATION:** St. Kitts and Nevis
- **LARGEST CITY:** Mexico City, Mexico (22.3 million people)

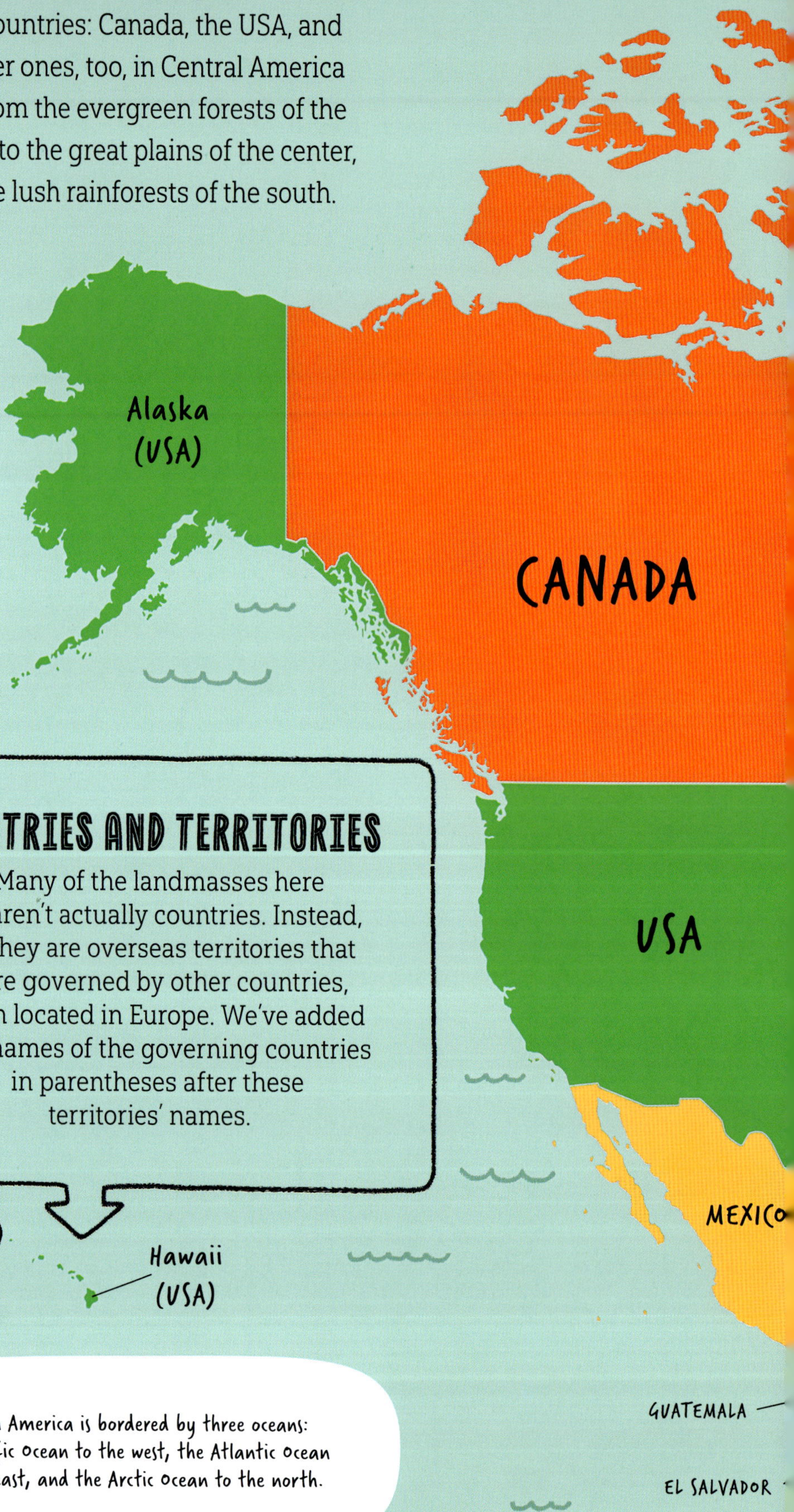

ARCTIC OCEAN
Alaska (USA)
CANADA
USA
MEXICO
Hawaii (USA)
GUATEMALA
EL SALVADOR
PACIFIC OCEAN

COUNTRIES AND TERRITORIES

Many of the landmasses here aren't actually countries. Instead, they are overseas territories that are governed by other countries, often located in Europe. We've added the names of the governing countries in parentheses after these territories' names.

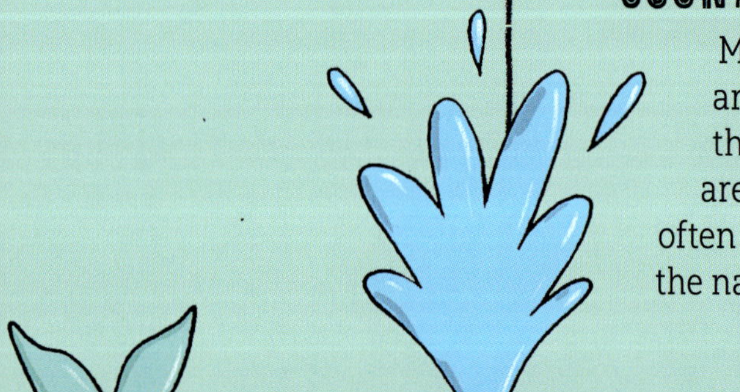

North America is bordered by three oceans: the Pacific Ocean to the west, the Atlantic Ocean to the east, and the Arctic Ocean to the north.

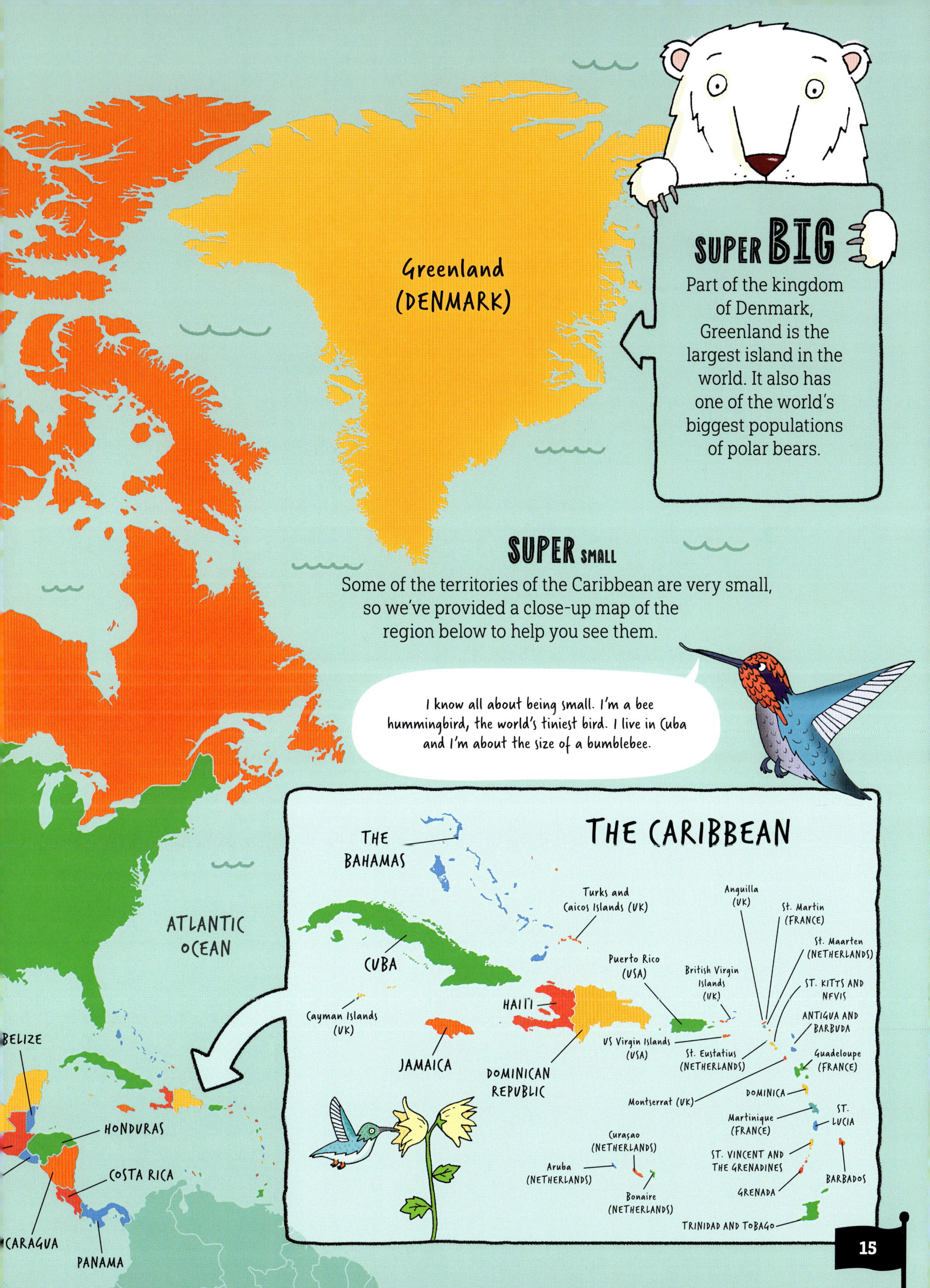

Greenland
(DENMARK)
SUPER BIG
Part of the kingdom of Denmark, Greenland is the largest island in the world. It also has one of the world's biggest populations of polar bears.
SUPER SMALL
Some of the territories of the Caribbean are very small, so we've provided a close-up map of the region below to help you see them.
I know all about being small. I'm a bee hummingbird, the world's tiniest bird. I live in Cuba and I'm about the size of a bumblebee.
ATLANTIC OCEAN
BELIZE
HONDURAS
COSTA RICA
CARAGUA
PANAMA
THE CARIBBEAN
THE BAHAMAS
CUBA
Cayman Islands (UK)
JAMAICA
HAITI
DOMINICAN REPUBLIC
Turks and Caicos Islands (UK)
Puerto Rico (USA)
British Virgin Islands (UK)
US Virgin Islands (USA)
Anguilla (UK)
St. Martin (FRANCE)
St. Maarten (NETHERLANDS)
ST. KITTS AND NEVIS
ANTIGUA AND BARBUDA
St. Eustatius (NETHERLANDS)
Guadeloupe (FRANCE)
Montserrat (UK)
DOMINICA
Martinique (FRANCE)
ST. LUCIA
ST. VINCENT AND THE GRENADINES
BARBADOS
GRENADA
TRINIDAD AND TOBAGO
Curaçao (NETHERLANDS)
Aruba (NETHERLANDS)
Bonaire (NETHERLANDS)

CANADA

POPULATION: 39 million

AREA: 3,855,100 sq mi (9,984,670 sq km)

CURRENCY: Canadian dollar

FLAG ADOPTED: 1965

FLAG FACT: The country's maple trees, symbolized by the red leaf on the flag, produce a sweet syrup that is harvested in vast quantities. Around 80 percent of the world's maple syrup comes from Canada.

USA

POPULATION: 342 million

AREA: 3,796,742 sq mi (9,833,517 sq km)

CURRENCY: US dollar

FLAG ADOPTED: 1777

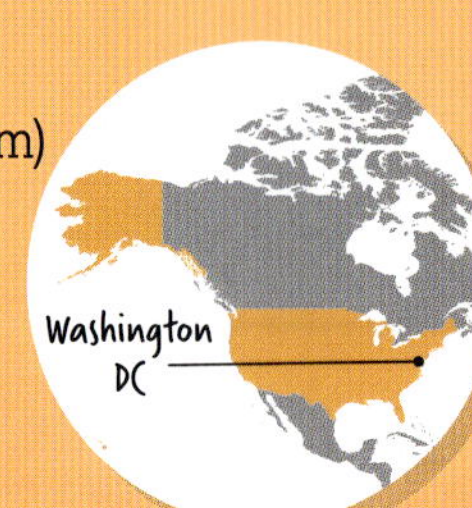

FLAG FACT: Unofficially known as the "Stars and Stripes" because of its distinctive design, the US flag is colored blue (to represent justice), white (to represent purity), and red (to represent bravery).

The US flag originally had just 13 stars, representing the 13 original states. As new states were created, more stars were added to the flag.

The first US flag is sometimes known as the "Betsy Ross" flag after the seamstress who, according to legend, came up with the design and sewed the very first version.

MEXICO

POPULATION: 131 million

AREA: 758,445 sq mi (1,964,375 sq km)

CURRENCY: Mexican peso

FLAG ADOPTED: 1821

Mexico City

FLAG FACT: The eagle on a cactus eating a snake is a symbol from Aztec legend, marking the spot where the city of Tenochtitlán (now Mexico City) was founded.

BELIZE

POPULATION: 416,000

AREA: 8,867 sq mi (22,966 sq km)

CURRENCY: Belize dollar

FLAG ADOPTED: 1981

Belmopan

FLAG FACT: The two figures on the Belizean flag are woodcutters, making Belize the only national flag to feature people as a major part of its design. The tree and motto *Sub umbrea floreo* ("I flourish in the shade") are references to the country's extensive rainforest.

GUATEMALA

POPULATION: 18.3 million

AREA: 42,042 sq mi (108,889 sq km)

CURRENCY: Quetzal

FLAG ADOPTED: 1871

Guatemala City

FLAG FACT: The multicolored bird featured on the flag is the resplendent quetzal, which has long played an important role in Guatemalan culture. It also gives its name to the country's currency.

HONDURAS

POPULATION: 9.5 million

AREA: 43,278 sq mi (112,090 sq km)

CURRENCY: Lempira

FLAG ADOPTED: 1866

FLAG FACT: Honduras borders the Caribbean Sea on its north coast and the Pacific Ocean on its southern coast. The blue bands on the country's flag symbolize these two bodies of water.

EL SALVADOR

POPULATION: 6.6 million

AREA: 8,124 sq mi (21,041 sq km)

CURRENCY: US dollar

FLAG ADOPTED: 1912

San Salvador

FLAG FACT: The triangle at the flag's center contains images of the country's seas and volcanoes. Poking up is a golden staff holding a red hat, representing liberty, and, above that, a rainbow of peace.

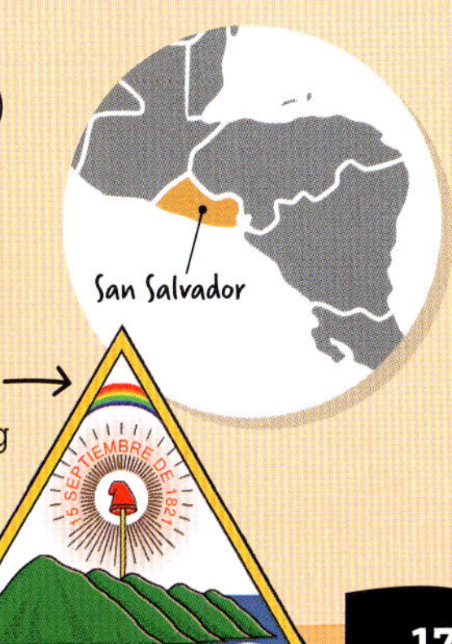

NICARAGUA

POPULATION: 6.7 million
AREA: 50,340 sq mi (130,370 sq km)
CURRENCY: Córdoba
FLAG ADOPTED: 1908

FLAG FACT: Nicaragua's flag features five volcanoes. They represent the five countries—Nicaragua, Honduras, El Salvador, Costa Rica, and Guatemala—that used to make up the United Provinces of Central America.

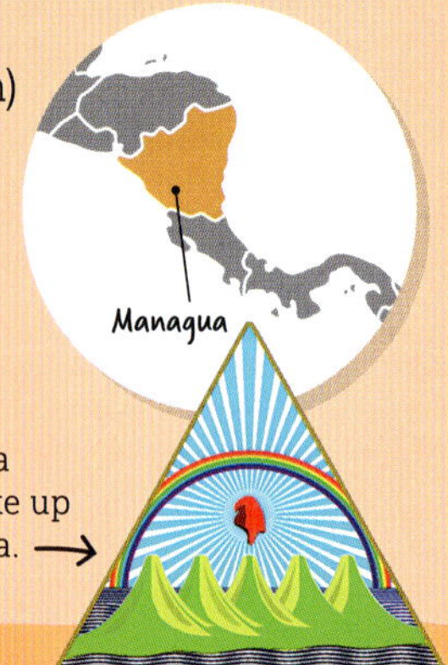

COSTA RICA

POPULATION: 5.3 million
AREA: 19,730 sq mi (51,100 sq km)
CURRENCY: Costa Rican colón
FLAG ADOPTED: 1848

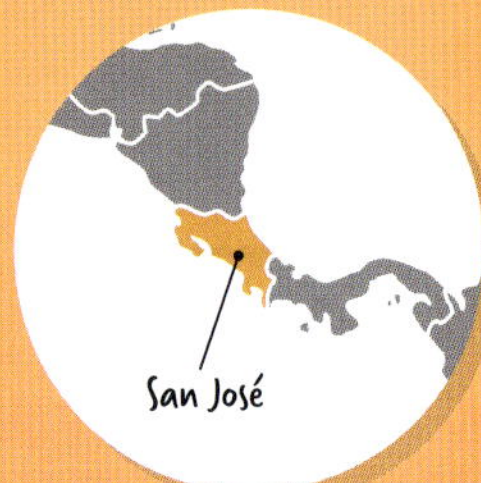

FLAG FACT: Spanish rule of Costa Rica ended in 1821. However, the country didn't become an independent country until 1838. Its current flag, adopted 10 years later, was based on the French flag (see p.41).

PANAMA

POPULATION: 4.5 million
AREA: 29,120 sq mi (75,420 sq km)
CURRENCY: Balboa/US dollar
FLAG ADOPTED: 1904

FLAG FACT: The red and blue colors on the flag stand for the colors of the country's two main political parties when the flag was first adopted. The white areas symbolize peace between the parties.

THE BAHAMAS

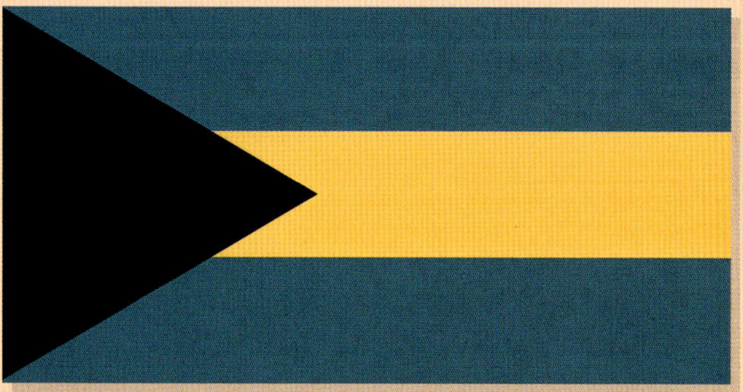

POPULATION: 411,000
AREA: 5,358 sq mi (13,880 sq km)
CURRENCY: Bahamian dollar
FLAG ADOPTED: 1973

FLAG FACT: The blue bands on the flag represent the clear-blue waters of the Caribbean Sea, while the yellow band represents the country's sandy beaches. The strength of the Bahamian people is symbolized by the black chevron (triangle).

CUBA

POPULATION: 11 million
AREA: 42,800 sq mi (110,860 sq km)
CURRENCY: Cuban peso
FLAG ADOPTED: 1902

FLAG FACT: The star on the Cuban flag is called La Estrella Solitaria ("the lone star") and symbolizes the country's freedom.

HAITI

POPULATION: 11.8 million
AREA: 10,714 sq mi (27,750 sq km)
CURRENCY: Haitian gourde
FLAG ADOPTED: 1986

FLAG FACT: At the center of the flag is the country's coat of arms, which features various objects, including a palm tree, a drum, and cannons.

DOMINICAN REPUBLIC

POPULATION: 10.8 million
AREA: 18,792 sq mi (48,670 sq km)
CURRENCY: Dominican peso
FLAG ADOPTED: 1844

FLAG FACT: The Dominican Republic is the only country in the world to feature a Bible on its flag. It's shown open, with three spears on either side.

JAMAICA

POPULATION: 2.8 million
AREA: 4,244 sq mi (10,991 sq km)
CURRENCY: Jamaican dollar
FLAG ADOPTED: 1962

FLAG FACT: The Jamaican flag is the only national flag that doesn't include red, white, or blue in its design.

ANTIGUA AND BARBUDA

POPULATION: 103,000

AREA: 171 sq mi (443 sq km)

CURRENCY: East Caribbean dollar

FLAG ADOPTED: 1967

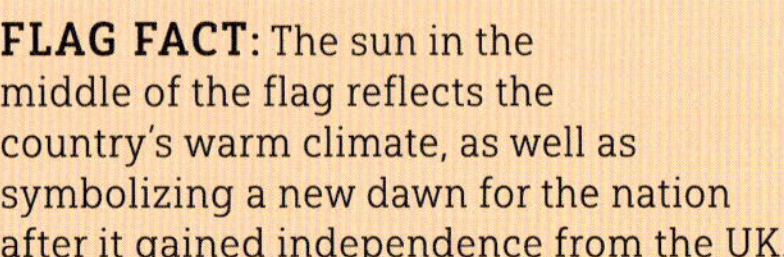

FLAG FACT: The sun in the middle of the flag reflects the country's warm climate, as well as symbolizing a new dawn for the nation after it gained independence from the UK.

SAINT KITTS AND NEVIS

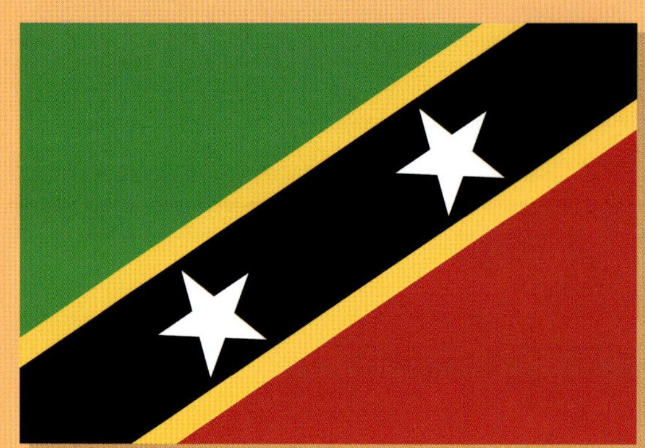

POPULATION: 55,000

AREA: 101 sq mi (261 sq km)
(Saint Kitts 65 sq mi [168 sq km];
Nevis 36 sq mi [93 sq km])

CURRENCY: East Caribbean dollar

FLAG ADOPTED: 1983

Basseterre

FLAG FACT: The two white stars on the flag represent the islands of Saint Kitts (which used to be called Saint Christopher) and Nevis. The flag was chosen following a competition held shortly before independence in 1983.

DOMINICA

POPULATION: 75,000

AREA: 290 sq mi (751 sq km)

CURRENCY: East Caribbean dollar

FLAG ADOPTED: 1978

Roseau

FLAG FACT: The flag features a sisserou parrot (also known as the imperial amazon parrot) in its center—this critically endangered parrot is found only on the island of Dominica and is the country's national bird.

SAINT LUCIA

POPULATION: 168,000

AREA: 238 sq mi (616 sq km)

CURRENCY: East Caribbean dollar

FLAG ADOPTED: 1967

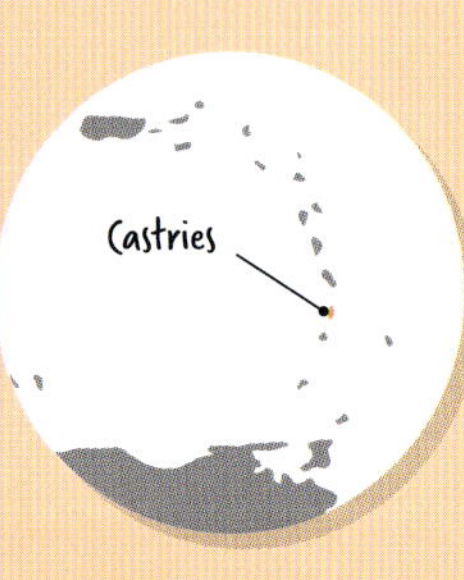

FLAG FACT: The yellow and black triangles in the middle of the flag represent two volcanic mountains (known as "Pitons"), which are famous landmarks on Saint Lucia.

SAINT VINCENT AND THE GRENADINES

POPULATION: 101,000

AREA: 150 sq mi (389 sq km)
(Saint Vincent 133 sq mi [344 sq km])

CURRENCY: East Caribbean dollar

FLAG ADOPTED: 1985

FLAG FACT: The three green diamonds in the middle of the flag are arranged in a V-shape (for Saint Vincent). The diamond shapes reflect how the island nation is often called "the Gem of the Antilles."

BARBADOS

POPULATION: 304,000

AREA: 166 sq mi (430 sq km)

CURRENCY: Barbadian dollar

FLAG ADOPTED: 1966

Bridgetown

FLAG FACT: In the middle of the flag is the head of a trident (a spear with three prongs). This symbolizes the country's independence and break with its past—when the country was a British colony, its flag featured a full trident.

GRENADA

POPULATION: 115,000

AREA: 133 sq mi (344 sq km)

CURRENCY: East Caribbean dollar

FLAG ADOPTED: 1974

St. George's

FLAG FACT: One of the island's main exports is nutmeg, a type of spice. The importance of the spice is reflected on the country's flag, which features a nutmeg pod on its left-hand side.

TRINIDAD AND TOBAGO

POPULATION: 1.4 million

AREA: 1,980 sq mi (5,128 sq km)

CURRENCY: Trinidad and Tobago dollar

FLAG ADOPTED: 1962

FLAG FACT: The colors represent earth (black), water (white), and fire (red). Red also stands for the warmth of the sun and the strength and friendliness of the nation's people.

PIRATE MAPS

Everyone knowns what a pirate map looks like—a hand-drawn island with a dotted line showing the route to a chest of buried treasure and an *X* marking the spot. The strange thing is—there's no evidence that pirates ever made maps. They were much more likely to spend the treasure they stole rather than carefully bury it and then mark its position on a map.

Volcanoes

TREASURE ISLAND

Treasure Island, an exciting tale of pirates and buried treasure, was written by Scottish author Robert Louis Stevenson and published in 1883. It included a hand-drawn map by Stevenson that has been the basis of every pirate map since.

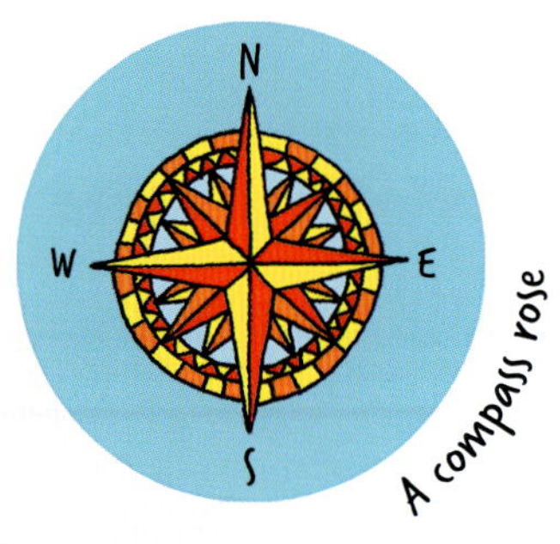

A compass rose

A treasure chest

A pirate ship

Most fictional pirate maps usually show the same features.

PIRATE FLAGS

Though pirate maps may not have existed, pirate flags definitely did. In the late 17th and early 18th centuries, pirate ships sailing in the Caribbean started flying flags to let other ships know that they were about to be attacked. There were lots of different designs, but most flags were either black or red and usually displayed terrifying images of skulls or devils.

THE JOLLY ROGER

According to some stories, early pirate ships flew a plain black flag to warn other ships to surrender their goods peacefully. If they didn't, the black flag would be switched to a red one, meaning that the pirates would take the goods by force. This red flag became known as the Jolie Rouge (meaning "pretty red"), which in time became "Jolly Roger." The name stuck even after the design of the flag changed.

An X marking the spot

OTHER PIRATE FLAGS

This is believed by some to be the flag of the most famous pirate of all, Edward Teach, better known as "Blackbeard" (c.1680–1718). It shows a skeleton holding a spear above a heart, which was intended to be a signal to any victims that the pirate would show them no mercy.

Bartholomew Roberts (c.1682–1722), or "Black Bart," was one of the most successful pirates. During his career, hc robbed more than 400 ships. When preparing to attack, legend says he flew the above flag, which shows a pirate holding an hourglass with a skeleton—a sign to his victims that he wasn't afraid of death.

Sea monsters

SOUTH AMERICA

The fourth-largest continent, South America is famed for its incredible landscapes, including dense rainforests, towering mountains, bone-dry deserts, great grassy plains, and, in the far south, enormous icy glaciers. It forms part of a wider region known as Latin America, where most of the people speak either Spanish or Portuguese.

SOUTH AMERICA FACTS

- **SIZE:** 6.9 million sq mi (17.8 million sq km)
- **NO. OF COUNTRIES:** 12
- **POPULATION:** 434 million
- **LARGEST COUNTRY BY AREA:** Brazil
- **LARGEST COUNTRY BY POPULATION:** Brazil
- **SMALLEST COUNTRY BY AREA AND POPULATION:** Suriname
- **LARGEST CITY:** São Paolo, Brazil (12 million people)

THE STUNNING SOUTH

South America is home to some incredible natural wonders, shown here on this physical map.

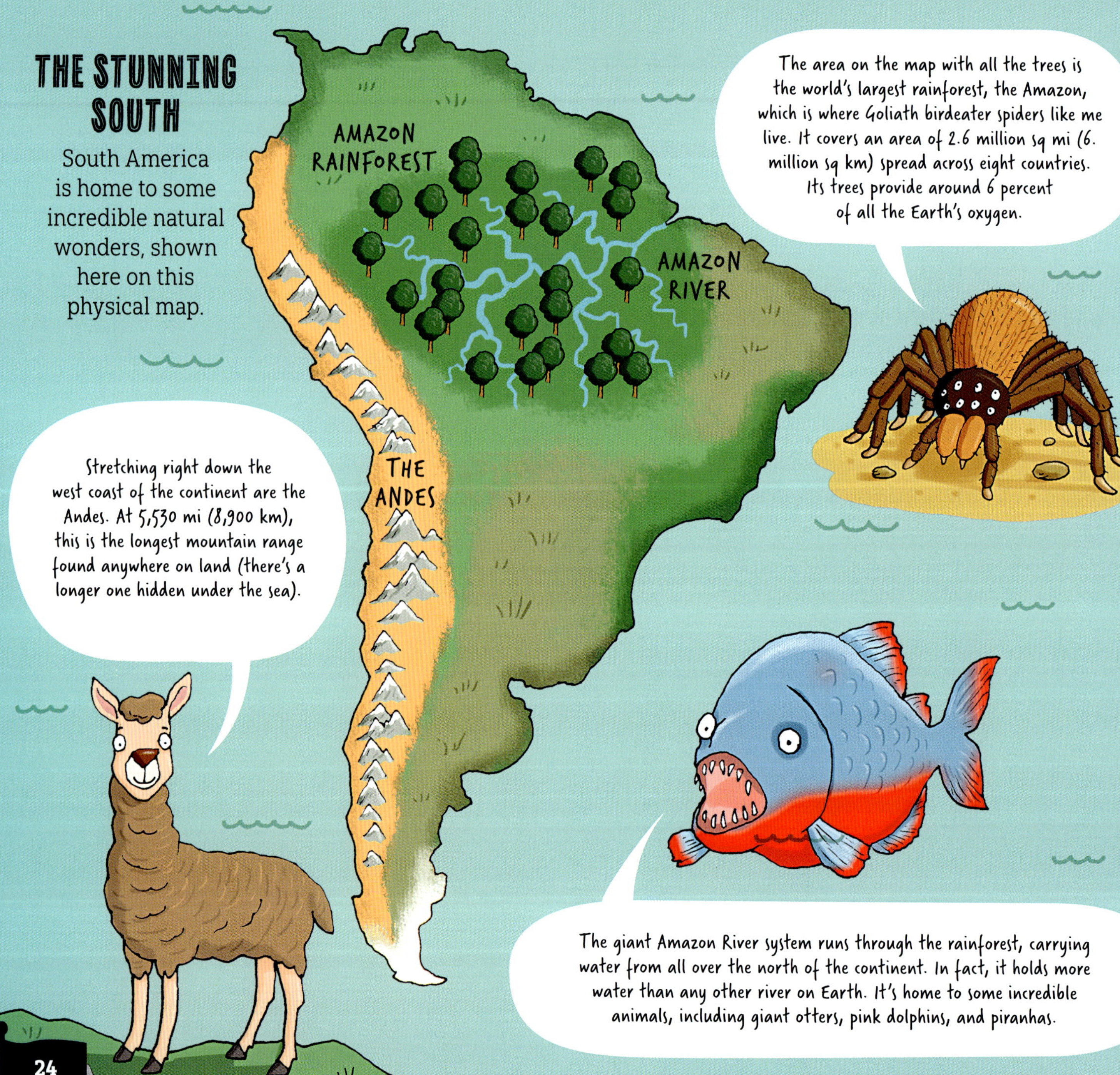

EUROPE IN AMERICA

This area, French Guiana, looks like a country of South America, but it's actually an overseas department of France. That means it is part of the European Union and its currency is the euro.

LANGUAGES

Many languages are spoken here, including English (the official language of Guyana), Dutch (the official language of Suriname), and countless Indigenous languages—spoken by the people who were here long before European settlers arrived. Nine countries have Spanish as their main language, but just one, Brazil, has Portuguese. However, because Brazil is so big, the number of Spanish speakers (around 214 million) is only slightly larger than the number of Portuguese speakers (around 211 million).

The Falkland Islands are an overseas territory of the UK. Argentina, which refers to the archipelago as the Islas Malvinas, disputes the UK's ownership and claims that the islands should belong to it instead.

VENEZUELA

POPULATION: 31 million

AREA: 352,140 sq mi (912,050 sq km)

CURRENCY: Venezuelan bolivar

FLAG ADOPTED: 2006

FLAG FACT: The flag used to have seven stars representing the seven original provinces of Venezuela. An eighth star, representing a later historic province, was added in 2006.

COLOMBIA

POPULATION: 50 million

AREA: 440,831 sq mi (1,138,910 sq km)

CURRENCY: Colombian peso

FLAG ADOPTED: 1861

FLAG FACT: Colombia's tricolor flag is unusual because its bands are different sizes. The yellow band (which represents the country's riches) takes up half of the flag, and the blue and red bands each fill a quarter.

ECUADOR

POPULATION: 18.3 million

AREA: 109,484 sq mi (283,561 sq km)

CURRENCY: US dollar

FLAG ADOPTED: 1860

FLAG FACT: The Ecuadorian flag features the country's coat of arms. On top sits an Andean condor—a massive bird of prey that is native to South America—and in the center is an image of Chimborazo, the highest mountain in Ecuador. →

Home to giant tortoises, penguins, and many other rare animal species, the Galápagos Islands are a province of Ecuador. The region has its own flag, which is a tricolor made up of green, white, and blue bands.

GUYANA

POPULATION: 794,000
AREA: 83,000 sq mi (214,969 sq km)
CURRENCY: Guyanese dollar
FLAG ADOPTED: 1966

Georgetown

FLAG FACT: You can see why this flag is nicknamed "the Golden Arrowhead." This striking design was created to honor the country's Indigenous Peoples as well as point to Guyana's bright future when it gained independence from the UK in the 1960s.

SURINAME

POPULATION: 647,000
AREA: 63,251 sq mi (163,820 sq km)
CURRENCY: Surinamese dollar
FLAG ADOPTED: 1975

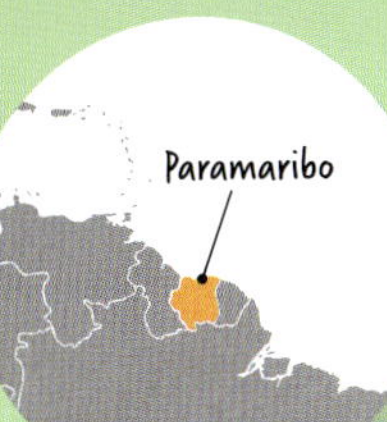

FLAG FACT: The colored bands on this flag represent the country's jungles (green), its progress (red), and freedom (white). The yellow star in the center stands for Suriname's united people and their "golden future."

BRAZIL

POPULATION: 220 million
AREA: 3,287,957 sq mi (8,515,770 sq km)
CURRENCY: Brazilian real
FLAG ADOPTED: 1889

Brasília

FLAG FACT: This is one of a handful of national flags where the design reflects the nation's shape; the yellow diamond featured in the middle roughly represents the outline of Brazil.

Green and yellow were originally chosen as the colors of Brazil because they were the colors of the Portuguese royal families who ruled the country in the early 1800s.

In the middle of the flag is a blue globe featuring 27 stars—one for each of the country's 26 states and its Federal District. The stars are arranged to reflect constellations that you can see above the country in the night sky.

PERU

POPULATION: 33 million
AREA: 496,225 sq mi (1,285,216 sq km)
CURRENCY: Sol
FLAG ADOPTED: 1825

FLAG FACT: Peru's flag sometimes features a coat of arms made up of three parts: a vicuña (a llama-like animal), a cinchona tree, and a cornucopia (horn) filled with gold and silver coins.

BOLIVIA

POPULATION: 12.3 million
AREA: 424,164 sq mi (1,098,581 sq km)
CURRENCY: Boliviano
FLAG ADOPTED: 1851

FLAG FACT: Bolivia's flag is made up of three equal horizontal bands (or fesses). The red band represents bravery, the yellow band symbolizes the country's mineral resources, and the green band stands for the nation's lush landscape.

Bolivia has a second official flag known as the Wiphala. It's a square made up of 49 smaller squares representing the Indigenous Peoples of the country.

CHILE

POPULATION: 18.7 million
AREA: 291,933 sq mi (756,102 sq km)
CURRENCY: Chilean peso
FLAG ADOPTED: 1817

FLAG FACT: The red band on Chile's flag represents the blood spilled in the country's fight for independence, the blue stands for the sky, and white symbolizes the snowcapped Andes mountains.

PARAGUAY

Front side (obverse)

Rear side (reverse)

POPULATION: 7.2 million

AREA: 157,048 sq mi (406,752 sq km)

CURRENCY: Guarani

FLAG ADOPTED: 1842

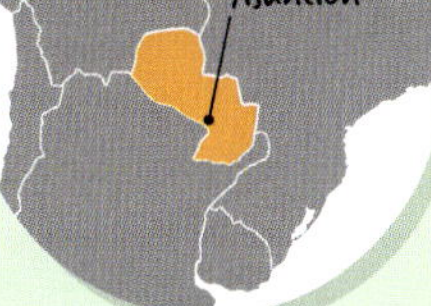

FLAG FACT: This is an unusual flag because it features a different emblem on each side. The "obverse" (front) side features the country's coat of arms while the "reverse" (back) side displays the seal of Paraguay's treasury.

URUGUAY

POPULATION: 3.4 million

AREA: 68,037 sq mi (176,215 sq km)

CURRENCY: Uruguayan peso

FLAG ADOPTED: 1830

Montevideo

FLAG FACT: Like Argentina, Uruguay also gained independence from Spain, and its flag features a similar design. The nine stripes on the flag represent the original departments of Uruguay.

ARGENTINA

POPULATION: 47 million

AREA: 1,073,500 sq mi (2,780,400 sq km)

CURRENCY: Argentine peso

FLAG ADOPTED: 1860

FLAG FACT: The three equal bands featured on Argentina's flag represent the blue of the skies and the white peaks of the Andes mountains.

The sun in the middle of the flag features a human face, which is thought to be based on the Inca god of the sun, Inti.

Nicknamed "the Sun of May," the emblem represents a moment during the May Revolution, which took place in 1810 in Buenos Aires (today, Argentina's capital city), when the sun broke through the clouds.

MAPS THROUGH TIME

Over time, maps have become much more accurate. The earliest maps showed only small, local areas. Gradually, the places being mapped became larger as people explored more regions and the technology for creating maps improved. After the late 15th century, European sailors began making long voyages of discovery, reaching lands they had never explored or mapped before.

AROUND THE WORLD

This map shows the route taken by the first expedition to sail right around the world, from 1519–1522.

People used to add pictures of monsters and strange creatures, like me, to maps to warn others about the dangers of unknown lands.

People had been living in the Americas for thousands of years before Europeans arrived. Until that point, the populations of each continent had no idea that the other existed.

JOURNEY OF TWO HALVES

The first journey to circumnavigate (travel around) the world set off in 1519 led by the Portuguese sailor Ferdinand Magellan. He died in 1521, and the expedition was completed under the command of one of the other sailors on the expedition, Juan Sebastián Elcano.

Magellan's Route
Elcano's Route

Antarctica is so remote that explorers didn't reach it until 1820. The first accurate maps of the continent weren't created until the 20th century.

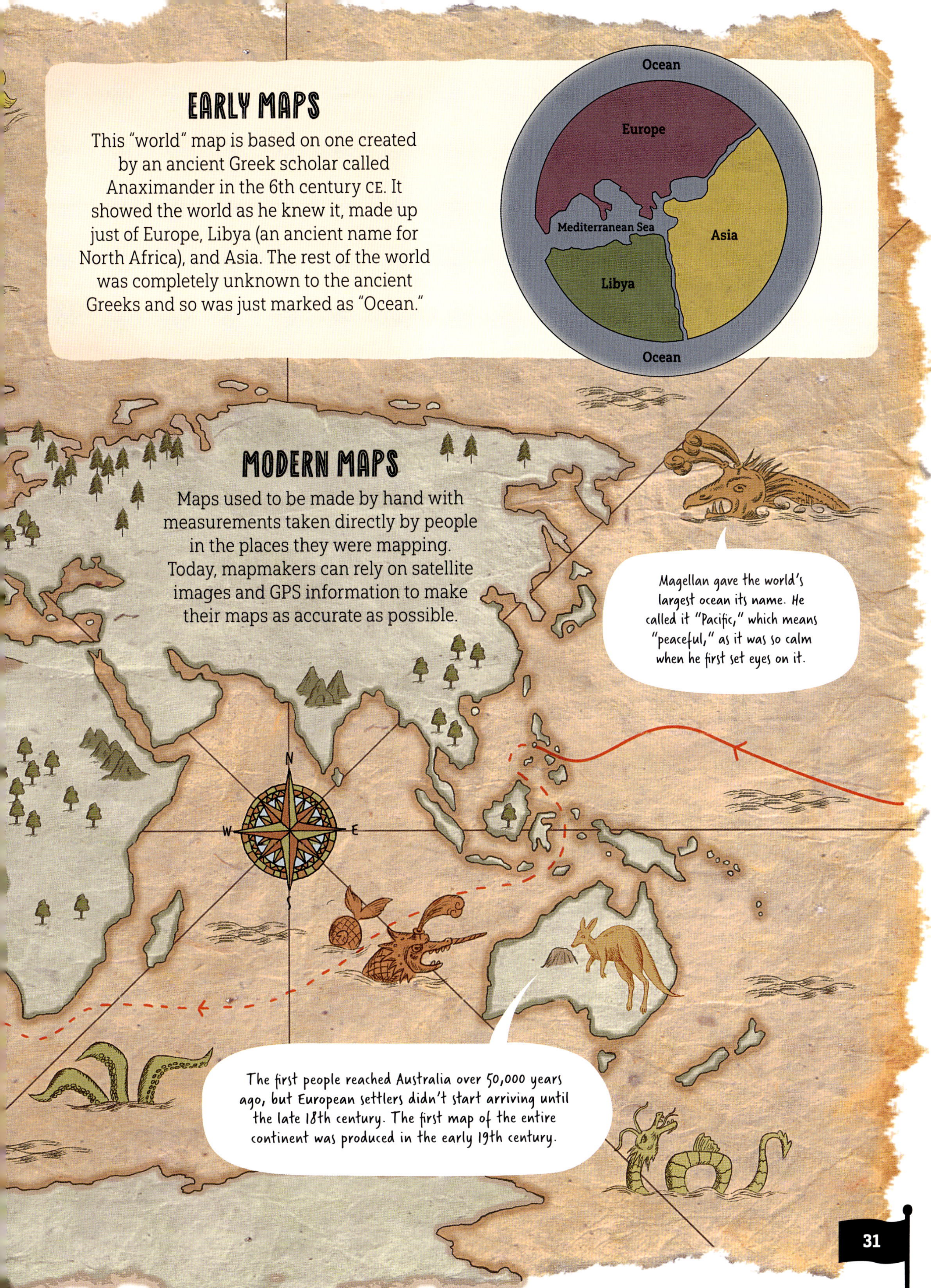

EARLY MAPS

This "world" map is based on one created by an ancient Greek scholar called Anaximander in the 6th century CE. It showed the world as he knew it, made up just of Europe, Libya (an ancient name for North Africa), and Asia. The rest of the world was completely unknown to the ancient Greeks and so was just marked as "Ocean."

MODERN MAPS

Maps used to be made by hand with measurements taken directly by people in the places they were mapping. Today, mapmakers can rely on satellite images and GPS information to make their maps as accurate as possible.

EUROPE

The second-smallest continent is packed with people, most of whom live in its many large cities. Away from urban areas, there are great stretches of forests in the north, mountain ranges in the center, and scorching scrubland in the south. Several countries border the Mediterranean Sea, which divides Europe from North Africa and Western Asia. Around the world, many people speak European languages as a result of the voyages of conquest and colonization that set out from here between the 15th and 19th centuries.

EUROPE FACTS

- **SIZE:** 3.9 million sq mi (10.2 million sq km)
- **NO. OF COUNTRIES:** 49
- **POPULATION:** 745 million
- **LARGEST COUNTRY BY AREA:** Russia (also partly in Asia)
- **LARGEST COUNTRY BY AREA WHOLLY IN EUROPE:** Ukraine
- **LARGEST COUNTRY BY POPULATION:** Russia (also partly in Asia)
- **LARGEST COUNTRY BY POPULATION WHOLLY IN EUROPE:** Germany
- **SMALLEST COUNTRY BY AREA AND POPULATION:** Vatican City
- **LARGEST CITY:** Moscow, Russia (19.1 million people)

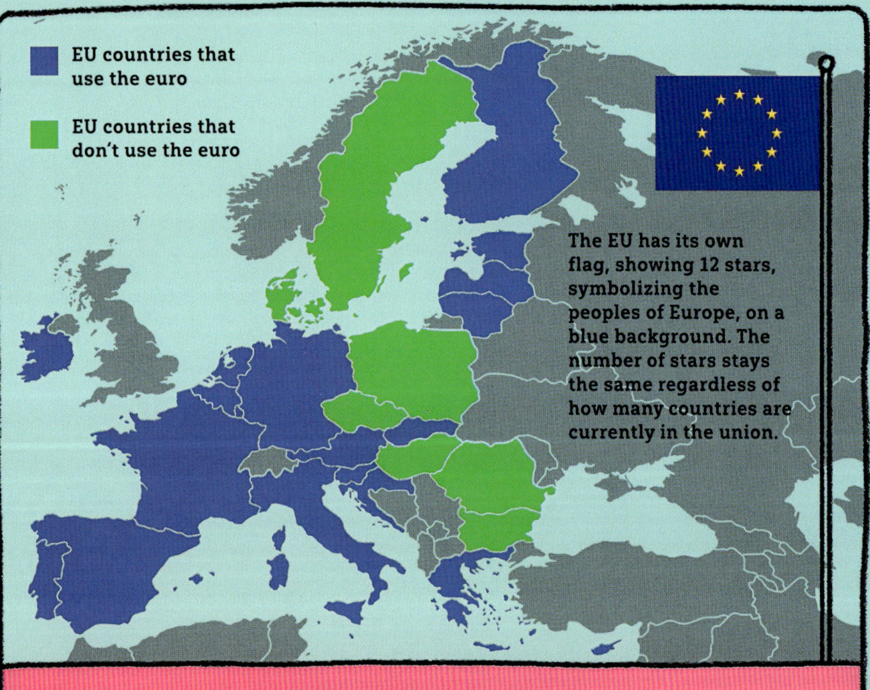

ICELAND

Four countries make up the United Kingdom: England, Scotland, Wales, and Northern Ireland. The UK used to be part of the EU but left following a nationwide vote in 2016.

POLITICAL UNION

Twenty-seven European countries are in a political confederation known as the European Union (EU). People in an EU country can travel to—and live and work in—any other EU country. Twenty members of the EU also share a currency, known as the euro. Six non-EU countries also use this currency: Andorra, Monaco, San Marino, Vatican City, Kosovo, and Montenegro.

LIECHTENSTEIN
SAN MARINO
ANDORRA
MONACO
VATICAN CITY
LITTLE LANDS
Europe is home to five countries that are too small to be seen on a map of the whole continent. Their rough positions are marked on the above map and include Earth's two smallest countries: Monaco, at roughly 0.77 sq mi (2 sq km), and the Vatican City, at just 1.7 sq mi (0.44 sq km).
Because Europe and Asia occupy the same landmass, the exact division between the two continents isn't always clear. The area of Russia west of the Ural Mountains is usually regarded as being in Europe, as is the part of Turkey west of the Black Sea. But Russia is generally grouped in Europe, while Turkey is considered part of Asia.
ATLANTIC OCEAN
SWEDEN
FINLAND
NORWAY
URAL MOUNTAINS
Faroe Islands (DENMARK)
ESTONIA
RUSSIA
LATVIA
DENMARK
Kaliningrad (RUSSIA)
LITHUANIA
NETHERLANDS
IRELAND
UNITED KINGDOM
BELARUS
POLAND
GERMANY
BELGIUM
CZECHIA
UKRAINE
LUXEMBOURG
SLOVAKIA
AUSTRIA
MOLDOVA
FRANCE
SWITZERLAND
HUNGARY
ROMANIA
CROATIA
ITALY
SLOVENIA
SERBIA
KOSOVO
BLACK SEA
BOSNIA AND HERZEGOVINA
BULGARIA
MONTENEGRO
TURKEY
SPAIN
NORTH MACEDONIA
ALBANIA
GREECE
TURKEY
PORTUGAL
Gibraltar (UK)
MALTA
CYPRUS

NORWAY

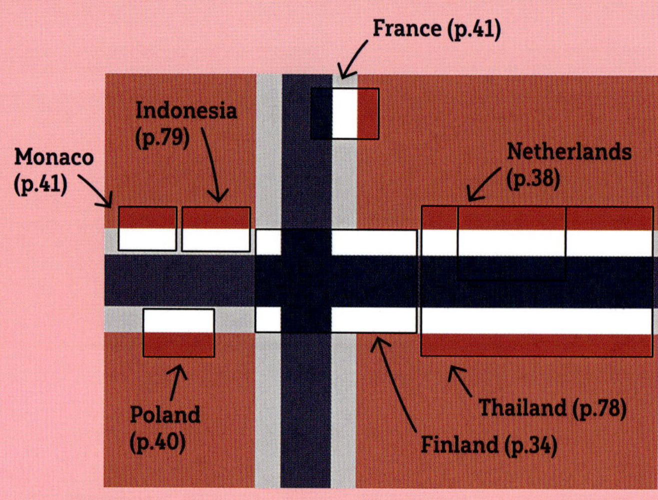

POPULATION: 5.5 million

AREA: 125,021 sq mi (323,802 sq km)

CURRENCY: Norwegian krone

FLAG ADOPTED: 1898

FLAG FACT: The Nordic countries are five nations in northern Europe that have strong historical and cultural links: Norway, Finland, Sweden, Denmark, and Iceland (p.37). All have a flag featuring an off-center "Nordic cross."

Norway's flag is sometimes referred to as "the mother of all flags." If you look closely, you can see seven other current national flags hidden inside it.

FINLAND

POPULATION: 5.6 million

AREA: 130,559 sq mi (338,145 sq km)

CURRENCY: Euro

FLAG ADOPTED: 1918

FLAG FACT: The blue color of the cross stands for Finland's lakes (the country has over 187,000), and the white background represents the snow that covers the land in winter.

SWEDEN

POPULATION: 10.6 million

AREA: 173,860 sq mi (450,295 sq km)

CURRENCY: Swedish krona

FLAG ADOPTED: 1906

FLAG FACT: The colors of Sweden's flag reflect the country's coat of arms, which features three golden crowns set on a blue background.

DENMARK

POPULATION: 6 million

AREA: 16,639 sq mi (43,094 sq km)

CURRENCY: Danish krone

FLAG ADOPTED: 1625

FLAG FACT: Known as the Dannebrog ("Danish cloth"), Denmark's national flag is the oldest continuously used flag in the world. According to legend, the flag fell from heaven during a battle in 1219. The red and white design was officially adopted as the country's flag in 1625.

ESTONIA

POPULATION: 1.2 million

AREA: 17,463 sq mi (45,228 sq km)

CURRENCY: Euro

FLAG ADOPTED: 1918
(and readopted in 1990)

FLAG FACT: The flags of the three Baltic nations, Estonia, Latvia, and Lithuania, were created when the countries became independent after World War I. However, they were replaced when the countries were taken over by the Soviet Union (see p.59), then readopted when the Soviet Union collapsed in the early 1990s.

LATVIA

POPULATION: 1.8 million

AREA: 24,938 sq mi (64,589 sq km)

CURRENCY: Euro

FLAG ADOPTED: 1923
(and readopted in 1990)

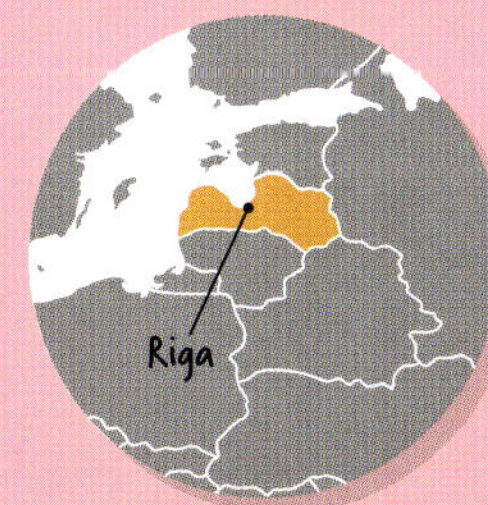

FLAG FACT: This red-and-white design has been traced back to Latvian tribes of the 1280s. It's said that the white represents a sheet that a dying warrior was laid on, and the red represents his blood.

LITHUANIA

POPULATION: 2.6 million

AREA: 25,200 sq mi (65,300 sq km)

CURRENCY: Euro

FLAG ADOPTED: 1922
(and readopted in 1989)

FLAG FACT: Yellow symbolizes freedom and wheat fields; green represents the country's forests and hope for the future; and red stands for courage and the blood spilled in defense of the homeland.

SCOTLAND

POPULATION: 5.4 million

AREA: 30,086 sq mi (77,925 sq km)

CURRENCY: British pound

FLAG ADOPTED: Not applicable (but design dates back to Middle Ages)

FLAG FACT: One of the world's oldest flags, it's been flown since at least the 14th century. However, it was replaced by the Union Jack (see opposite) as the offical flag in the early 18th century, though it is widely flown in the country.

NORTHERN IRELAND

POPULATION: 1.9 million

AREA: 5,236 sq mi (13,562 sq km)

CURRENCY: British pound

FLAG ADOPTED: Not applicable

FLAG FACT: Northern Ireland doesn't have an official flag, as there isn't a design that is agreed on by all its political parties. The Ulster Banner, shown here, was the flag of government from 1953 to 1972. It is still used by some sports teams, including the Northern Ireland football team.

ENGLAND

POPULATION: 57 million

AREA: 50,301 sq mi (130,278 sq km)

CURRENCY: British pound

FLAG ADOPTED: Not applicable

FLAG FACT: The flag showing the red cross of St. George has been regarded as the country's flag since the 13th century. It was incorporated into the Union Jack in the early 18th century (see opposite), since when it has not been an official national flag (though lots of people still fly it).

WALES

POPULATION: 3.1 million

AREA: 8,006 sq mi (20,735 sq km)

CURRENCY: British pound

FLAG ADOPTED: 1959

FLAG FACT: The Red Dragon (or Y Ddraig Goch in Welsh) has been used as a symbol of Wales for centuries. The first king of the Tudor dynasty, Henry VII, who was Welsh, carried a standard bearing a dragon during his invasion of England in 1485.

UNITED KINGDOM

POPULATION: 68 million
AREA: 93,629 sq mi (242,500 sq km)
CURRENCY: British pound
FLAG ADOPTED: 1801

London

FLAG FACT: The Union Jack (or Union Flag) is the flag that represents the entire nation of the United Kingdom, which is made up of the four countries: England, Scotland, Wales, and Northern Ireland.

The flag was devised under James I, the first king of both England and Scotland. It mixed the flags of England and Scotland, but not Wales, as it didn't have its own flag at that time. An old flag of Ireland was added later.

Ireland was once part of the UK, but the Republic of Ireland is now an independent country, and it's just Northern Ireland that remains within the union.

IRELAND

POPULATION: 5.2 million
AREA: 27,133 sq mi (70,273 sq km)
CURRENCY: Euro
FLAG ADOPTED: 1937

FLAG FACT: After Ireland broke free of the UK in the 1920s, this flag was designed to try to build peace between its still feuding communities. The green represents the country's Catholics, the orange its Protestants, and the white stands for a peaceful union between the two.

ICELAND

POPULATION: 364,000
AREA: 39,600 sq mi (103,000 sq km)
CURRENCY: Icelandic króna
FLAG ADOPTED: 1915

FLAG FACT: Iceland's flag looks much like that of Denmark (see p.35), which ruled this island until 1944. The blue on the flag represents the surrounding Atlantic Ocean.

NETHERLANDS

POPULATION: 17.8 million
AREA: 16,040 sq mi (41,543 sq km)
CURRENCY: Euro
FLAG ADOPTED: 1937

FLAG FACT: This flag has its origins in the 1570s, when it was a tricolor of orange (the color of the Dutch royal family), white, and blue. Today, an orange pennant (a narrow, triangular flag) is flown with the national flag during royal birthdays.

BELGIUM

POPULATION: 12 million
AREA: 11,787 sq mi (30,528 sq km)
CURRENCY: Euro
FLAG ADOPTED: 1831

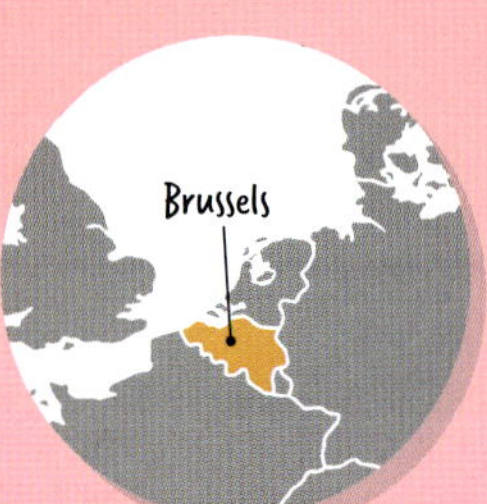

FLAG FACT: Belgium gained independence from the Netherlands in the 1830s, at which point it changed its flag from having horizontal bands (like the Dutch one) to vertical ones.

The design of the Belgian flag was based on France's (see p.41), while its colors were inspired by the coat of arms of an old region called Brabant. This featured a gold lion with a red tongue and claws set on a black background.

LUXEMBOURG

POPULATION: 671,000
AREA: 998 sq mi (2,586 sq km)
CURRENCY: Euro
FLAG ADOPTED: 1845
(readopted in 1972)

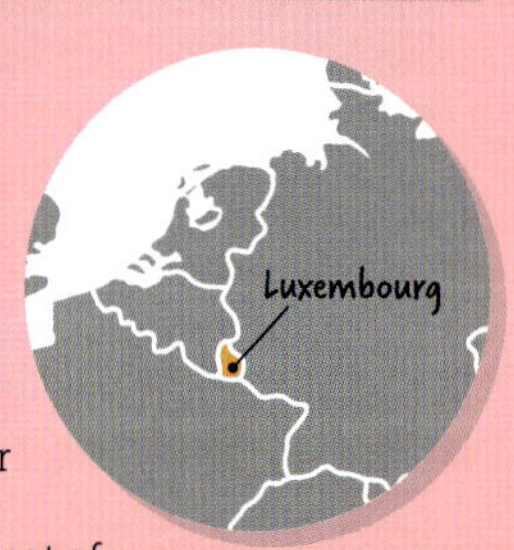

FLAG FACT: This flag looks very similar to the one for the Netherlands, but with lighter colors. The colors come from the coat of arms of the grand duke of Luxembourg, the country's head of state.

BELARUS

POPULATION: 9.5 million
AREA: 80,200 sq mi (207,600 sq km)
CURRENCY: Belarusian ruble
FLAG ADOPTED: 1995

FLAG FACT: Belarus's flag features a vertical band with a red-and-white geometric pattern. This design is found on the blouses and skirts that are worn as part of the country's national costume.

UKRAINE

POPULATION: 36 million
AREA: 233,032 sq mi (603,550 sq km)
CURRENCY: Ukrainian hryvnia
FLAG ADOPTED: 1918
(readopted in 1992)

FLAG FACT: The colors of Ukraine's flag originally came from a coat of arms but they gradually gained a different symbolism: the blue represents the skies and the yellow stands for the country's golden wheat fields.

MOLDOVA

POPULATION: 3.6 million
AREA: 13,070 sq mi (33,851 sq km)
CURRENCY: Moldovan leu
FLAG ADOPTED: 1990

FLAG FACT: In the middle of the Moldovan flag is the country's coat of arms, featuring the head of an aurochs, a type of wild cattle that once roamed across Europe and Asia but died out in the 1600s.

ROMANIA

POPULATION: 18.1 million
AREA: 92,043 sq mi (238,391 sq km)
CURRENCY: Romanian leu
FLAG ADOPTED: 1989

FLAG FACT: Romania was formed by combining two regions called Walachia (represented by the yellow stripe) and Moldavia (the blue stripe). A red stripe was added because it featured on the flags of both regions. Moldova used to be part of Romania, and the two countries have the same colors on their flags.

GERMANY

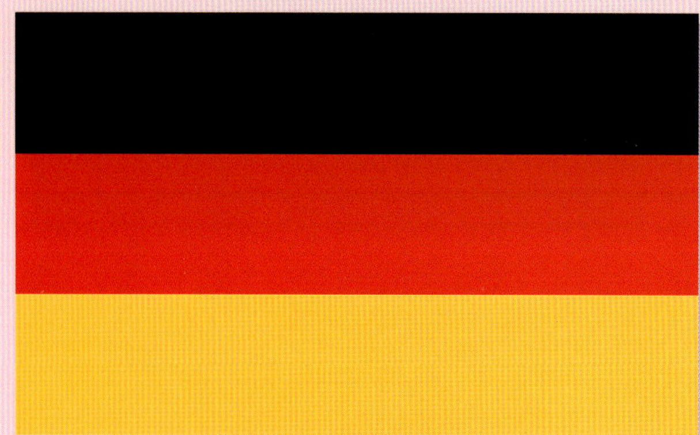

POPULATION: 84 million

AREA: 138,070 sq mi (357,022 sq km)

CURRENCY: Euro

FLAG ADOPTED: 1949
(since 1990 for reunified country)

FLAG FACT: The flag was first adopted in 1919 but was replaced in the 1930s by the swastika, the symbol of the Nazis who then controlled Germany. It was readopted after World War II and the defeat of the Nazis.

POLAND

POPULATION: 39 million

AREA: 120,728 sq mi (312,685 sq km)

CURRENCY: Złoty

FLAG ADOPTED: 1919

FLAG FACT: Poland's flag is very similar to that of both Monaco (see opposite) and Indonesia (p.79). Red and white are the official colors of Poland and feature on its coat of arms.

SWITZERLAND

POPULATION: 8.9 million

AREA: 15,937 sq mi (41,277 sq km)

CURRENCY: Swiss franc

FLAG ADOPTED: 1889

FLAG FACT: The flag's cross design dates back to the Middle Ages, when it featured on standards carried into battle by Swiss soldiers. It's one of just two square-shaped national flags (the other is the Vatican City; see p.43).

LIECHTENSTEIN

POPULATION: 40,300

AREA: 62 sq mi (160 sq km)

CURRENCY: Swiss franc

FLAG ADOPTED: 1937

FLAG FACT: Liechtenstein's flag is very similar to that of Haiti (see p.19). This was realized at the 1936 Olympics and led to the addition of the gold crown—a reference to the prince who is the head of state of this tiny nation.

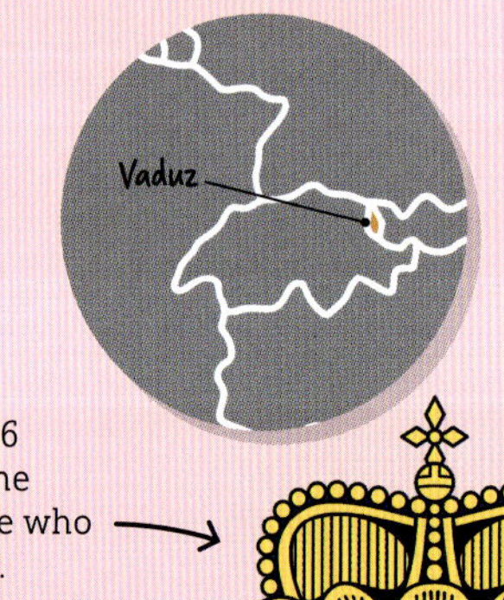

FRANCE

POPULATION: 66 million
AREA: 212,900 sq mi (551,500 sq km)
CURRENCY: Euro
FLAG ADOPTED: 1794

FLAG FACT: France's flag, known as the Tricolore (meaning "three colors") was adopted during the French Revolution when the country's monarchy was overthrown. The three bands stand for the ideals of the revolution: liberty, equality, and fraternity.

France has a number of overseas territories, including five "departments" that are regarded as being integral parts of France with the same status as the mainland in Europe. Each has its own unofficial flag.

French Guiana (see p.25)

Guadeloupe (see p.15)

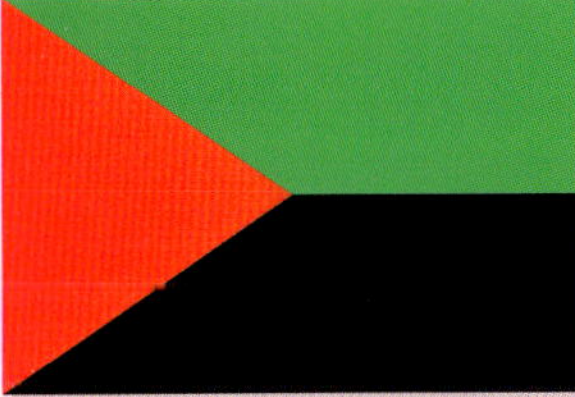

Martinique (see p.15)

Mayotte (see p.51)

Réunion (see p.51)

MONACO

POPULATION: 31,800
AREA: 0.8 sq mi (2 sq km)
CURRENCY: Euro
FLAG ADOPTED: 1881

FLAG FACT: The flag shows the colors of the Grimaldis, the royal family who have ruled this tiny country since the 1200s. The flag looks almost identical to that of Indonesia (see p.79) but has a slightly different ratio: 4:5 rather than 2:3 (see p.10).

ANDORRA

POPULATION: 85,000
AREA: 181 sq mi (468 sq km)
CURRENCY: Euro
FLAG ADOPTED: 1866
(coat of arms added 1993)

FLAG FACT: This tiny country's flag has three bands of colors (the central yellow is slightly wider than the others), and a coat of arms featuring a bishop's hat and a pair of red cows.

CZECHIA

POPULATION: 10.8 million

AREA: 30,451 sq mi (78,867 sq km)

CURRENCY: Czech koruna

FLAG ADOPTED: 1992
(adopted for Czechoslovakia in 1920)

Prague

FLAG FACT: Czechia used to be part of a larger country, Czechoslovakia. When that split into two countries in 1993, Czechia (then the Czech Republic) kept the old flag of Czechoslovakia, while Slovakia adopted a new flag (see right).

SLOVAKIA

POPULATION: 5.6 million

AREA: 18,933 sq mi (49,035 sq km)

CURRENCY: Euro

FLAG ADOPTED: 1993

Bratislava

FLAG FACT: Slovakia's flag looks very similar to Russia's (see p.45) but has the country's coat of arms on the left. This features a white double cross rising above three blue mounds. These represent the country's religion, Christianity, and the region's mountainous landscape.

AUSTRIA

POPULATION: 9 million

AREA: 32,383 sq mi (83,871 sq km)

CURRENCY: Euro

FLAG ADOPTED: 1945

Vienna

FLAG FACT: Austria's flag is based on a very old design, first used on the flag of Frederick II, Duke of Austria, in 1230. It wasn't formally adopted as the country's flag until after World War II.

HUNGARY

POPULATION: 9.9 million

AREA: 35,918 sq mi (93,028 sq km)

CURRENCY: Forint

FLAG ADOPTED: 1957

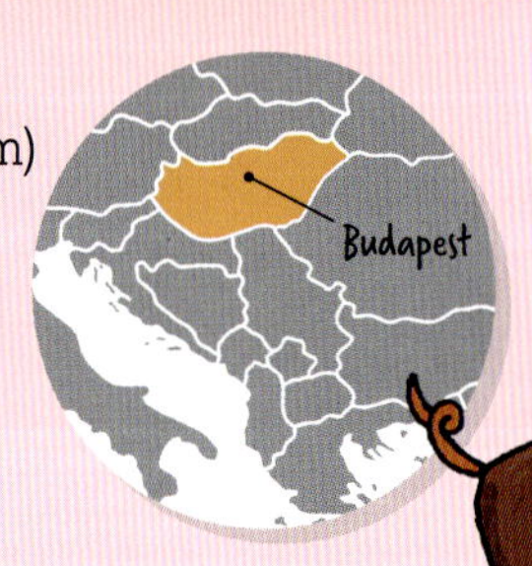

FLAG FACT: The flag pattern first emerged during a failed 1848–1849 revolution in Hungary against its then rulers, the Hapsburg Empire.

ITALY

POPULATION: 61 million
AREA: 116,350 sq mi (301,340 sq km)
CURRENCY: Euro
FLAG ADOPTED: 1946

Rome

FLAG FACT: Italy's flag was invented around the time of the French Revolution in the 18th century and was based on the colors of the French flag (see p.41)—but with green replacing blue.

Italy was once made up of several states and didn't become a single country until 1861. Its flag then was similar to today's but had a royal coat of arms and a crown, as Italy was ruled by a monarch at the time.

SAN MARINO

POPULATION: 35,000
AREA: 24 sq mi (61 sq km)
CURRENCY: Euro
FLAG ADOPTED: 2011
(originally adopted in 19th century)

FLAG FACT: The tiny country of San Marino lies entirely enclosed by Italy. In the past, it was protected from invasion by three castles, which today feature on the flag's coat of arms.

VATICAN CITY

POPULATION: 1,000
AREA: 0.17 sq mi (0.44 sq km)
CURRENCY: Euro
FLAG ADOPTED: 1929

Vatican City

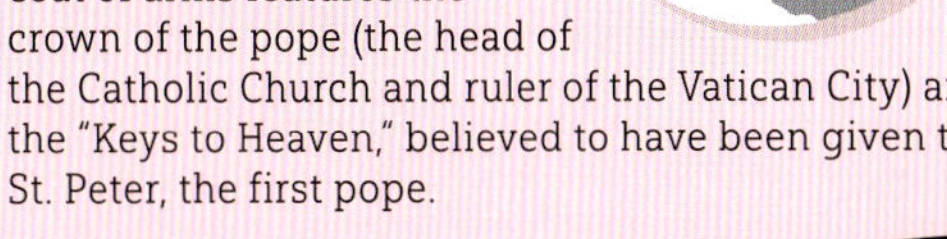

FLAG FACT: The flag's coat of arms features the crown of the pope (the head of the Catholic Church and ruler of the Vatican City) and the "Keys to Heaven," believed to have been given to St. Peter, the first pope.

SLOVENIA

POPULATION: 2.1 million

AREA: 7,906 sq mi (20,273 sq km)

CURRENCY: Euro

FLAG ADOPTED: 1991

Ljubljana

FLAG FACT: As with many other countries from this region, known as the Balkans, Slovenia's flag is red, white, and blue—also known as "Pan-Slavic" colors. These were inspired by Russia's flag. The coat of arms on the flag shows Mount Triglav, the country's highest mountain.

CROATIA

POPULATION: 4.2 million

AREA: 21,851 sq mi (56,594 sq km)

CURRENCY: Euro

FLAG ADOPTED: 1990

Zagreb

FLAG FACT: At the center of Croatia's flag is its coat of arms, featuring a shield of red and white checks. Above that is a crown of five smaller shields, which represent historic parts of the country.

SERBIA

POPULATION: 6.7 million

AREA: 29,913 sq mi (77,474 sq km)

CURRENCY: Serbian dinar

FLAG ADOPTED: 2006

Belgrade

FLAG FACT: Serbia's flag shows its coat of arms, featuring a two-headed white eagle, a national symbol.

KOSOVO

POPULATION: 2 million

AREA: 4,203 sq mi (10,887 sq km)

CURRENCY: Euro

FLAG ADOPTED: 2008

Pristina

FLAG FACT: Inspired by the European Union's flag (see p.32), Kosovo's design shows an outline of the country in the center, with six stars above it representing its six main ethnic communities—Albanians, Bosniaks, Gorani, Roma, Serbs, and Turks.

BOSNIA AND HERZEGOVINA

POPULATION: 3.8 million

AREA: 19,767 sq mi (51,197 sq km)

CURRENCY: Bosnia-Herzegovina convertible marka

FLAG ADOPTED: 1998

FLAG FACT: On this flag, the stars represent Europe, while the three points of the yellow triangle stand for the country's three main ethnic communities—Bosniaks, Croats, and Serbs.

MONTENEGRO

POPULATION: 600,000

AREA: 5,333 sq mi (13,812 sq km)

CURRENCY: Euro

FLAG ADOPTED: 2004

FLAG FACT: Montenegro's flag is based on a historic royal banner and features the coat of arms of a dynasty that once ruled the country.

NORTH MACEDONIA

POPULATION: 2.1 million

AREA: 9,928 sq mi (25,713 sq km)

CURRENCY: Macedonian denar

FLAG ADOPTED: 1995

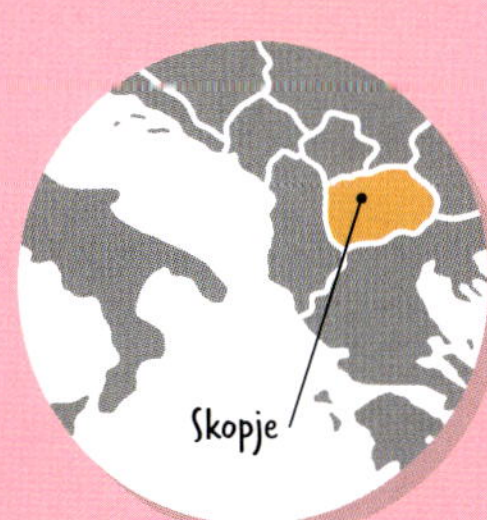

FLAG FACT: Like Slovenia, Croatia, Serbia, Kosovo, Bosnia and Herzegovina, and Montenegro, North Macedonia used to be part of a country called Yugoslavia, from which it became independent in 1991. The sun design on the flag symbolizes a new start for the country.

RUSSIA

POPULATION: 141 million

AREA: 6,601,665 sq mi (17,098,242 sq km)

CURRENCY: Russian ruble

FLAG ADOPTED: 1991

Moscow

FLAG FACT: During the 1600s, the country's ruler, Peter the Great, picked a flag for the new Russian navy that looked very similar to that of the Netherlands (see p.38), which he had just visited. It proved so popular, it was adopted as Russia's national flag.

BULGARIA

POPULATION: 6.8 million

AREA: 42,810 sq mi (110,879 sq km)

CURRENCY: Bulgarian lev

FLAG ADOPTED: 1990 (originally adopted in 1879)

FLAG FACT: The Bulgarian tricolor was inspired by Russia's flag (see p.45), with blue changed to green. The white is said to stand for peace, the red for bravery, and the green for the country's lush landscape and agriculture.

ALBANIA

POPULATION: 3.1 million

AREA: 11,100 sq mi (28,748 sq km)

CURRENCY: Albanian lek

FLAG ADOPTED: 1993

FLAG FACT: Albania's flag is a tribute to a 15th-century warrior called George Castriot, who fought for his country's independence and whose emblem was a black double-headed eagle.

GREECE

POPULATION: 10.5 million

AREA: 50,949 sq mi (131,957 sq km)

CURRENCY: Euro

FLAG ADOPTED: 1978

FLAG FACT: White and blue are the traditional colors of Greece—white represents purity, and blue symbolizes the country's sparkling seas and skies.

CYPRUS

POPULATION: 1.3 million

AREA: 3,572 sq mi (9,251 sq km)

CURRENCY: Euro

FLAG ADOPTED: 1960

FLAG FACT: Cyprus is one of only two countries in the world that feature maps on their flags (the other is Kosovo; see p.44). The image of Cyprus on the flag is colored copper-orange as a reference to the island's copper resources (Cyprus means "isle of copper").

SPAIN

POPULATION: 47 million
AREA: 195,124 sq mi (505,370 sq km)
CURRENCY: Euro
FLAG ADOPTED: 1981

Madrid

FLAG FACT: Spain's flag is made up of red and yellow bands, the traditional Spanish colors. On the left is the country's coat of arms, which represents the Spanish royal family as well as a number of smaller kingdoms that were unified to create the modern nation.

PORTUGAL

POPULATION: 10.2 million
AREA: 35,560 sq mi (92,090 sq km)
CURRENCY: Euro
FLAG ADOPTED: 1911

Lisbon

FLAG FACT: The modern Portuguese flag was invented when the country abolished its monarchy in the early 20th century. However, the Portuguese Shield, a sign of the monarchy dating back to the 13th century, was kept at the flag's center as a sign of continuity.

MALTA

POPULATION: 470,000
AREA: 122 sq mi (316 sq km)
CURRENCY: Euro
FLAG ADOPTED: 1964

Valletta

FLAG FACT: Malta's flag includes the George Cross in its top left corner—this medal was awarded by the British king to the Maltese people for their bravery during World War II.

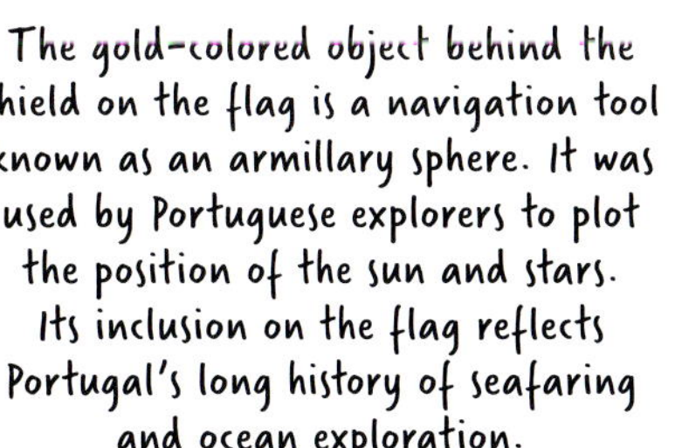

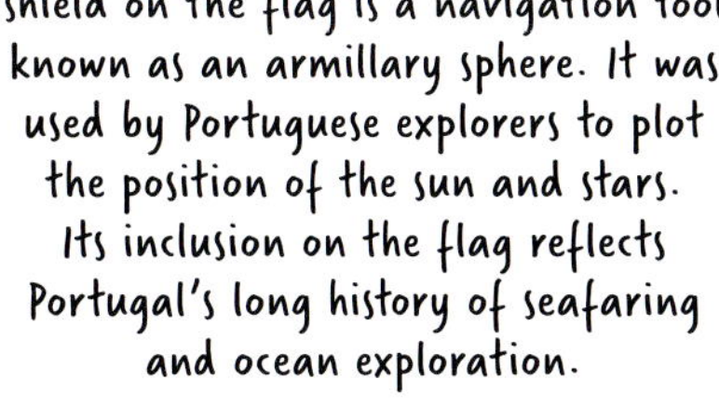

The gold-colored object behind the shield on the flag is a navigation tool known as an armillary sphere. It was used by Portuguese explorers to plot the position of the sun and stars. Its inclusion on the flag reflects Portugal's long history of seafaring and ocean exploration.

TRANSPORTATION MAPS

Maps not only show us where things are, they can also show us where to go and how to get from one place to another. Transportation maps focus on the routes between places, rather than the places themselves. These types of maps can show everything from local bus and train routes to major roads in a country or even flight paths across the whole world.

PUBLIC TRANSPORTATION MAPS

Many public transportation (or transit) systems, such as railroads, subways, and buses, use color-coded maps like the one below left. They show how different transportation routes in a system interconnect. This type of map is known as a schematic and it isn't supposed to be realistic. The distances and directions between stations have been changed to make the map as easy to read as possible. No surface features have been included.

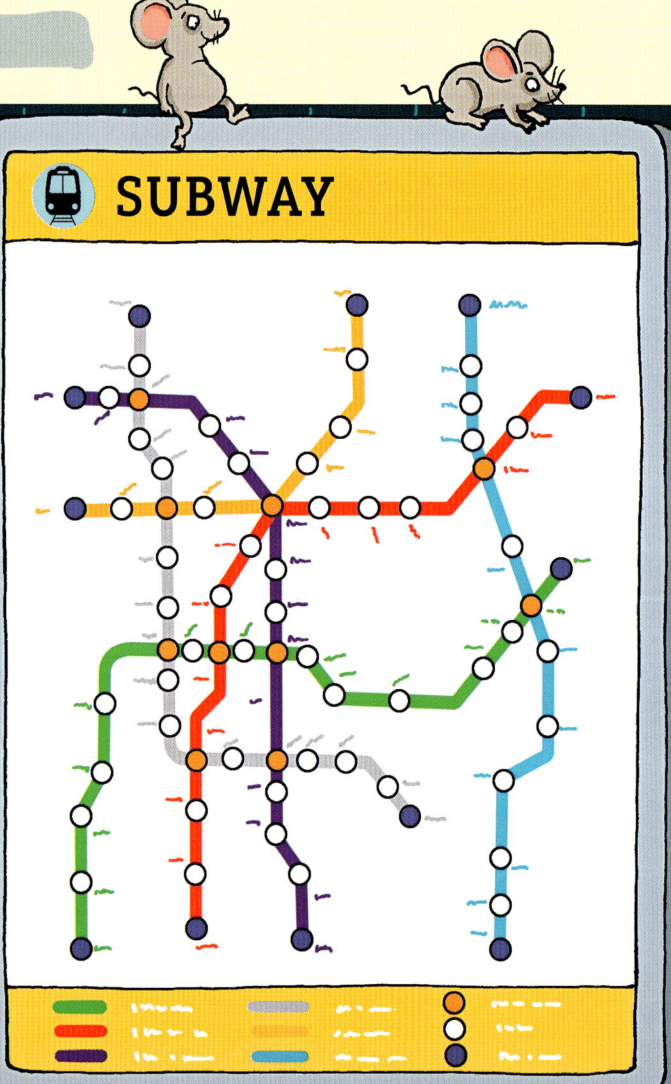

EXIT→

Each subway line has been given a separate color to make it clear where it goes. Every station is marked with a circle. Blue circles mark the end of a line, while orange circles mark transfer stations—places where two or more lines meet.

FLYING, DRIVING, AND SAILING

There are many other types of transportation maps, including ones that show major roads, shipping lanes, or even plane flight paths, such as the one below. All are designed to clearly show routes that vehicles take to get from one place to another.

PHONE MAPS

Transportation maps are some of the most commonly used maps, particularly on cell phones. Mapping apps allow you to plan journeys and to find out routes and distances. They can also guide you to your destination using audio commands.

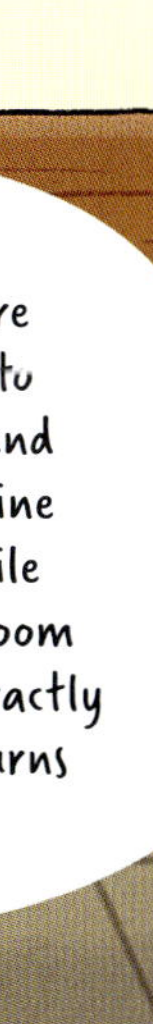

On a phone map, there are usually location markers to show your beginning and end points, and a highlighted line indicating your route. While you're traveling, you can zoom right in on the map to see exactly where you are and which turns you need to make.

AFRICA

Africa has more countries than any other continent. It also boasts some incredible natural wonders, including the Earth's biggest hot desert, the world's longest river, and the planet's largest land animals. There are plenty of people, too. In fact, Africa has the fastest-growing population of any continent.

AFRICA FACTS

- **SIZE:** 11.7 million sq mi (30.4 million sq km)
- **NO. OF COUNTRIES:** 54
- **POPULATION:** 1.4 billion
- **LARGEST COUNTRY BY AREA:** Algeria
- **LARGEST COUNTRY BY POPULATION:** Nigeria
- **SMALLEST COUNTRY BY AREA AND POPULATION:** Seychelles
- **LARGEST CITY:** Cairo (22.2 million people)

GO WITH THE FLOW

The Nile, the world's longest river, flows from Central Africa up to the far north of the continent, where it empties into the Mediterranean Sea. On its way, it winds for over 4,132 mi (6,650 km) and passes through—or alongside—10 countries.

SEA OF SAND

The orange area on the map below is the world's largest hot desert, the Sahara. It covers an area of 3.6 million sq mi (9.2 million sq km), which is about the same size as the USA—that's a lot of sand!

The grasslands of Eastern and Southern Africa are home to the world's biggest bird, the ostrich, the world's tallest animal, the giraffe, and the biggest animal of them all, the African elephant—that's me!

The world's second-largest tropical jungle (after the Amazon; see p.24), the Congo Rainforest covers around 0.8 million sq mi (2 million sq km) of Central Africa. It's the green area on this map. Its dense mass of trees hides many animals, including chimpanzees and gorillas.

STRANGE STATUS

Western Sahara is not officially recognized as a country. Much of it is occupied by Morocco. But the Sahrawi people of the area control around a third of the land, which they call the Sahrawi Arab Democratic Republic.

OLD AND NEW

Africa has been home to some of the world's earliest civilizations. Egypt can trace its history back thousands of years to the time of the pharaohs. The continent is also where you'll find the world's newest country, South Sudan, which became independent in 2011.

Madeira (PORTUGAL)
Canary Islands (SPAIN)
Western Sahara (disputed)
CABO VERDE
THE GAMBIA
GUINEA-BISSAU
SIERRA LEONE
LIBERIA
TOGO
EQUATORIAL GUINEA
SÃO TOMÉ AND PRÍNCIPE
REPUBLIC OF THE CONGO
MOROCCO
ALGERIA
TUNISIA
LIBYA
EGYPT
MAURITANIA
MALI
NIGER
CHAD
SUDAN
ERITREA
DJIBOUTI
SENEGAL
GUINEA
BURKINA FASO
BENIN
NIGERIA
CÔTE D'IVOIRE
GHANA
CAMEROON
CENTRAL AFRICAN REPUBLIC
SOUTH SUDAN
ETHIOPIA
SOMALIA
INDIAN OCEAN
RWANDA
UGANDA
KENYA
GABON
DEMOCRATIC REPUBLIC OF THE CONGO
BURUNDI
TANZANIA
SEYCHELLES
COMOROS
Mayotte (FRANCE)
MOZAMBIQUE
ANGOLA
ZAMBIA
MALAWI
MADAGASCAR
MAURITIUS
ATLANTIC OCEAN
ZIMBABWE
NAMIBIA
BOTSWANA
Réunion (FRANCE)
ESWATINI
LESOTHO
SOUTH AFRICA

AFRICAN UNION

This is the flag of the African Union, which is a political body that promotes peace and economic cooperation between the continent's countries.

The fourth-largest island in the world, Madagascar broke away from the African mainland around 180 million years ago. Since then, it's developed a diverse range of animals, many of which are found nowhere else on Earth, including lemurs and panther chameleons.

MOROCCO

POPULATION: 37 million
AREA: 276,662 sq mi (716,550 sq km)
CURRENCY: Moroccan dirham
FLAG ADOPTED: 1915

Rabat

FLAG FACT: The flag shows a green "Seal of Solomon," a five-pointed star that supposedly adorned a magical ring given by God to King Solomon of ancient Israel—an important figure in the Islamic traditions of the country.

ALGERIA

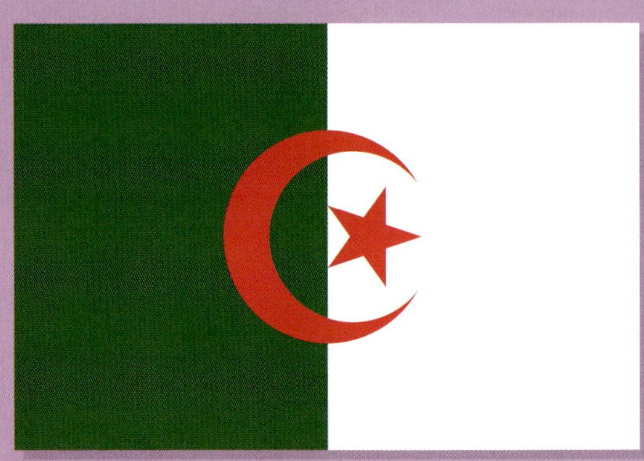

POPULATION: 47 million
AREA: 919,590 sq mi (2,381,740 sq km)
CURRENCY: Algerian dinar
FLAG ADOPTED: 1962

Algiers

FLAG FACT: Algeria's flag shows a star and crescent, symbols of Islam, North Africa's main religion. They're colored red to represent the blood shed during the country's struggle for independence from France between 1954 and 1964.

TUNISIA

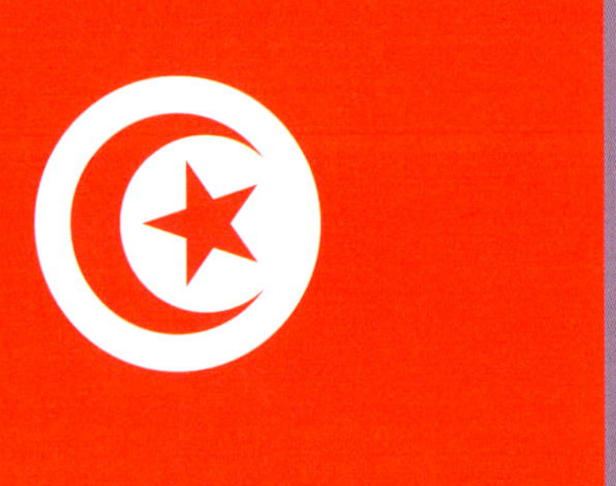

POPULATION: 12 million
AREA: 63,170 sq mi (163,610 sq km)
CURRENCY: Tunisian dinar
FLAG ADOPTED: 1827

Tunis

FLAG FACT: Tunisia's flag was designed in 1827 when the country was part of the Ottoman Empire. The flag continued to be flown when the country was controlled by France from 1881–1956, and became the official flag of an independent Tunisia in 1959.

LIBYA

POPULATION: 7.4 million
AREA: 679,362 sq mi (1,759,540 sq km)
CURRENCY: Libyan dinar
FLAG ADOPTED: 1951
(readopted in 2011)

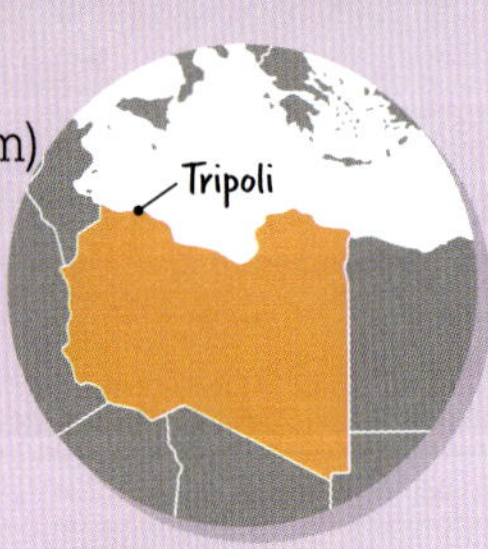

FLAG FACT: Libya's flag was first adopted when the country became independent from Italy in 1951. It was replaced from 1969–2011 when the dictator Muammar al-Gaddafi took over the country, but readopted following Gaddafi's overthrow.

EGYPT

POPULATION: 111 million
AREA: 386,000 sq mi (1,001,450 sq km)
CURRENCY: Egyptian pound
FLAG ADOPTED: 1984
(original design: 1952)

FLAG FACT: The flag's colors signify oppression (black) overcome by struggle (red) leading to peace (white). The golden eagle is the symbol of Saladin, a powerful sultan (ruler) of Egypt in the 12th century.

CABO VERDE

POPULATION: 611,000
AREA: 1,557 sq mi (4,033 sq km)
CURRENCY: Cape Verdean escudo
FLAG ADOPTED: 1992

FLAG FACT: The 10 stars on the flag represent the main islands of the nation, which is located off the west coast of Africa. The stripes signify peace (white), struggle (red), and the surrounding ocean (blue).

MAURITANIA

POPULATION: 4.3 million
AREA: 397,955 sq mi (1,030,700 sq km)
CURRENCY: Ouguiya
FLAG ADOPTED: 2017
(previous version: 1959)

FLAG FACT: This was once one of just two national flags not to contain the colors red, white, or blue (the other is Jamaica's; see p.19). But in 2017, red stripes were added to signify the country's ongoing struggle. Green represents Islam and yellow the Sahara Desert.

MALI

POPULATION: 22 million
AREA: 478,841 sq mi (1,240,192 sq km)
CURRENCY: West African CFA franc
FLAG ADOPTED: 1961

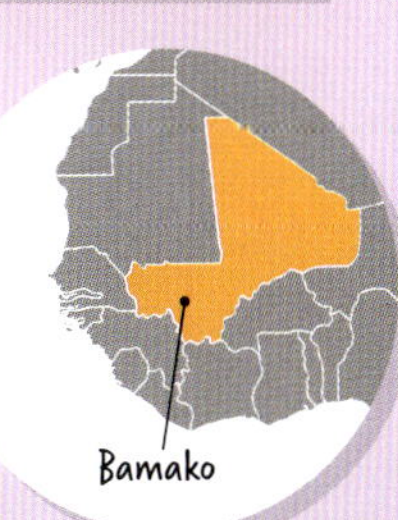

FLAG FACT: Red, gold, and green (along with black), shown here, are known as "Pan-African" colors and were adopted on many flags in the post-colonial era as symbols of African pride, freedom, and unity.

NIGER

POPULATION: 26 million

AREA: 489,191 sq mi (1,267,000 sq km)

CURRENCY: West African CFA franc

FLAG ADOPTED: 1959

Niamey

FLAG FACT: Niger's flag partly reflects its geography. Orange stands for the desert areas of the north, while green represents the more fertile area in the south. White stands for peace, on which sits an orange circle representing the sun.

CHAD

POPULATION: 19.1 million

AREA: 495,755 sq mi (1,284,000 sq km)

CURRENCY: Central African CFA franc

FLAG ADOPTED: 1959

N'Djamena

FLAG FACT: Chad's flag is almost identical to that of Romania's (see p.39), though Chad's blue stripe is very slightly darker. Blue stands for the sky, gold for desert (the Sahara covers much of the country's north), and red for the struggle for independence.

SUDAN

POPULATION: 50 million

AREA: 668,602 sq mi (1,861,484 sq km)

CURRENCY: Sudanese pound

FLAG ADOPTED: 1970

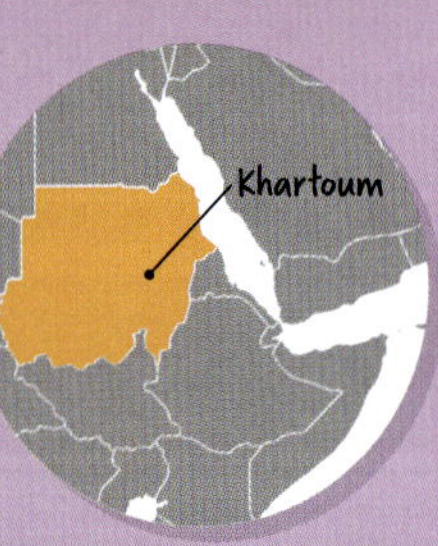

FLAG FACT: As with several countries in North Africa and the Middle East, Sudan's flag features red, white, black, and green. These are known as "Pan-Arab" colors, shown here, and their use signifies a desire for unity between Arab nations.

SOUTH SUDAN

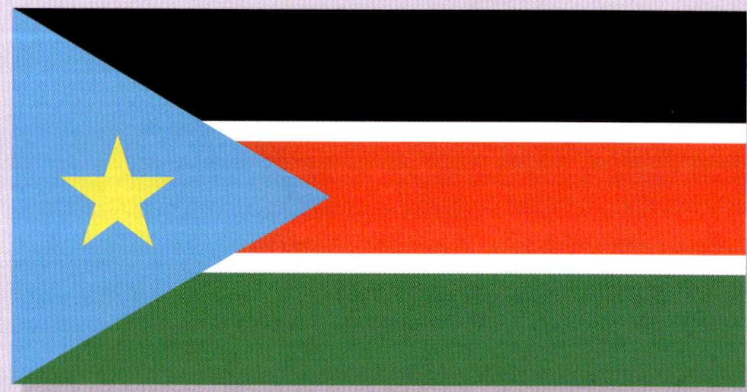

POPULATION: 12.7 million

AREA: 248,777 sq mi (644,329 sq km)

CURRENCY: South Sudanese pound

FLAG ADOPTED: 2011

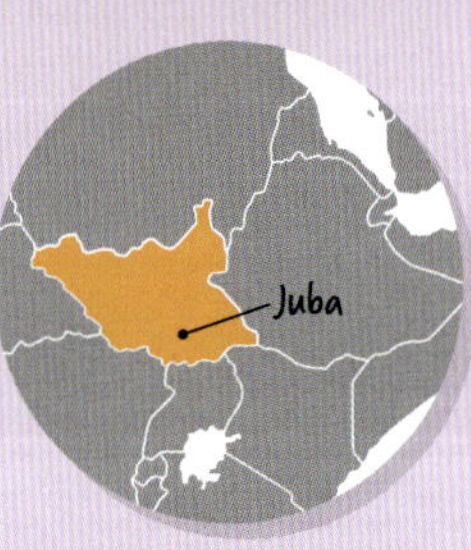

FLAG FACT: South Sudan's flag looks similar to that of its northern neighbor, Sudan, from which it broke away in 2011 following a civil war. The star was added to symbolize hope and success for the new country's future.

SENEGAL

POPULATION: 18.8 million

AREA: 75,955 sq mi (196,722 sq km)

CURRENCY: West African CFA franc

FLAG ADOPTED: 1960

FLAG FACT: The flag is very similar to that of Mali (see p.53), as, for two months in 1960 after breaking free of French rule, the two countries were joined together. However, they soon split apart, whereupon Senegal added a green star to its version of the flag.

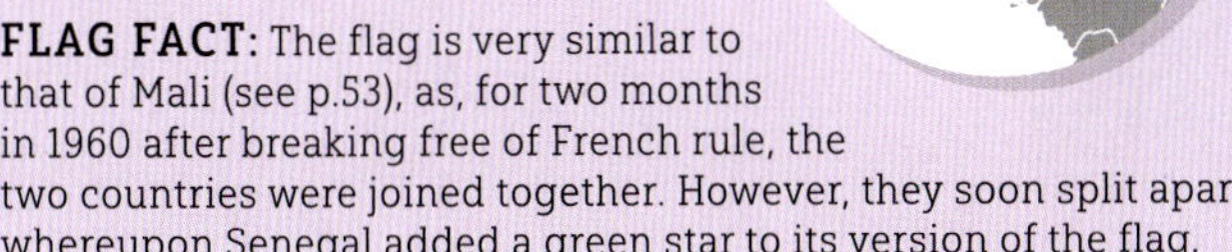

THE GAMBIA

POPULATION: 2.5 million

AREA: 4,400 sq mi (11,300 sq km)

CURRENCY: Gambian dalasi

FLAG ADOPTED: 1965

FLAG FACT: The bands represent the Gambia river (blue), agriculture (green), the sun (red), and peace (white). When Gambia was a British colony from 1880–1965, its flag featured a coat of arms with an elephant and a palm tree.

GUINEA-BISSAU

POPULATION: 2.1 million

AREA: 13,948 sq mi (36,125 sq km)

CURRENCY: West African CFA franc

FLAG ADOPTED: 1974

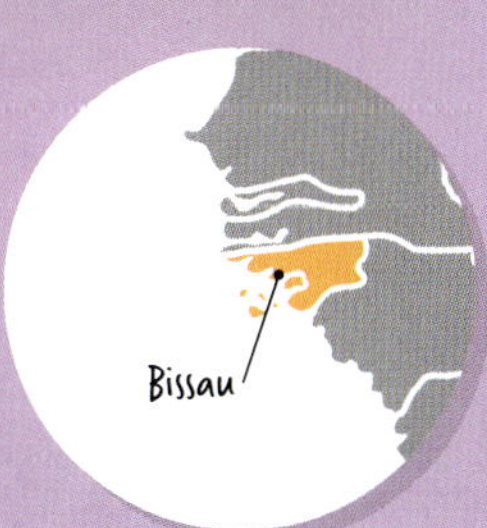

FLAG FACT: The country's flag looks much like its neighbor Ghana's (see p.57), with the same Pan-African colors (see p.53) in a slightly different arrangement. It also features a black star, which became a symbol of African pride in the 20th century.

GUINEA

POPULATION: 14 million

AREA: 94,926 sq mi (245,857 sq km)

CURRENCY: Guinean franc

FLAG ADOPTED: 1958

FLAG FACT: As with Guinea-Bissau and many other flags of this region, Guinea's features the Pan-African colors of red, yellow, and green, symbolizing unity across the continent (see p.53).

SIERRA LEONE

POPULATION: 9.1 million

AREA: 27,699 sq mi (71,740 sq km)

CURRENCY: Leone

FLAG ADOPTED: 1961

FLAG FACT: The three colored bands on Sierra Leone's flag stand for the country's natural resources (green), unity and justice (white), and the large natural harbor located by the capital, Freetown (blue).

LIBERIA

POPULATION: 5.4 million

AREA: 43,000 sq mi (111,369 sq km)

CURRENCY: Liberian dollar

FLAG ADOPTED: 1847

FLAG FACT: A former US colony, Liberia's flag resembles the USA's (see p.16), but has just one star rather than fifty. The flag is flown by many ships from other countries so as to avoid paying taxes in those countries. These are known as "flags of convenience."

CÔTE D'IVOIRE

POPULATION: 30 million

AREA: 124,503 sq mi (322,463 sq km)

CURRENCY: West African CFA franc

FLAG ADOPTED: 1959

FLAG FACT: The Côte d'Ivoire's flag's design is based on the country's former colonial power, France (see p.41). The vertical colors are identical to those on the flag of Ireland (see p.37), but are in a different order.

BURKINA FASO

POPULATION: 23 million

AREA: 105,870 sq mi (274,200 sq km)

CURRENCY: West African CFA franc

FLAG ADOPTED: 1984

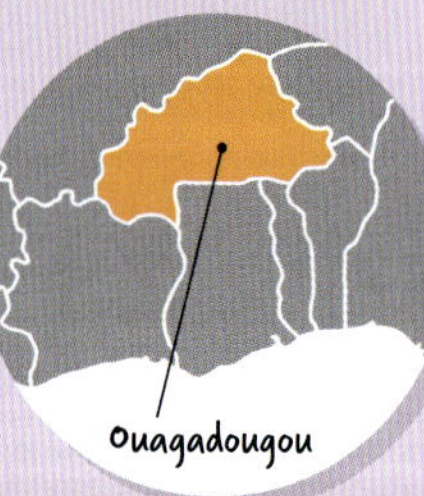

FLAG FACT: The flag was adopted in the 1980s when the country of Upper Volta changed its name to Burkina Faso (meaning "land of honest men"). It uses the Pan-African colors, which are displayed on several other African flags (see p.53).

GHANA

POPULATION: 35 million

AREA: 92,098 sq mi (238,533 sq km)

CURRENCY: Cedi

FLAG ADOPTED: 1957

FLAG FACT: Ghana was the second country to use the Pan-African colors for its flag, after Ethiopia (see p.60). It has a black star at its center, another Pan-African symbol, and its design influenced the flag of Guinea-Bissau (see p.55).

TOGO

POPULATION: 8.9 million

AREA: 21,925 sq mi (56,785 sq km)

CURRENCY: West African CFA franc

FLAG ADOPTED: 1960

FLAG FACT: The flag was designed by the Togolese artist Paul Ahyi and looks similar to Liberia's flag (see opposite), but uses the Pan-African colors of red, yellow, and green.

BENIN

POPULATION: 14.7 million

AREA: 43,484 sq mi (112,622 sq km)

CURRENCY: West African CFA franc

FLAG ADOPTED: 1959

FLAG FACT: Adopted following independence from France, the flag was replaced from 1975–1990, when Benin was a communist country. It was changed back after the collapse of the Soviet Union (see p.59).

NIGERIA

POPULATION: 237 million

AREA: 356,669 sq mi (923,768 sq km)

CURRENCY: Naira

FLAG ADOPTED: 1960

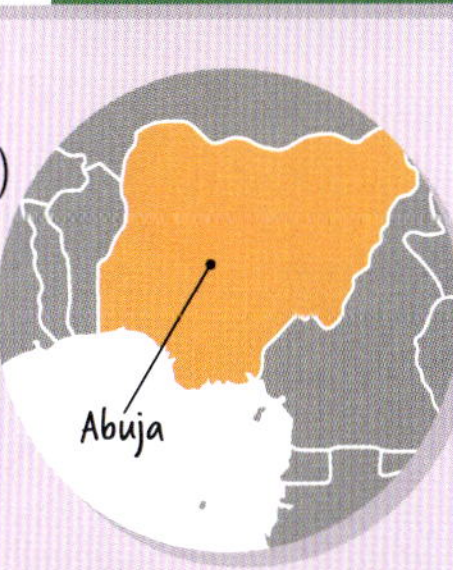

FLAG FACT: This was chosen as the winner of a competition to design a flag for the newly independent country in 1960. The original design included a red sun, but that was later removed.

CAMEROON

POPULATION: 31 million

AREA: 183,570 sq mi (475,440 sq km)

CURRENCY: West African CFA franc

FLAG ADOPTED: 1975

Yaoundé

FLAG FACT: The Cameroonian flag was designed in 1957, three years before the country became independent from the UK and France. A yellow star signifying unity was added in 1975.

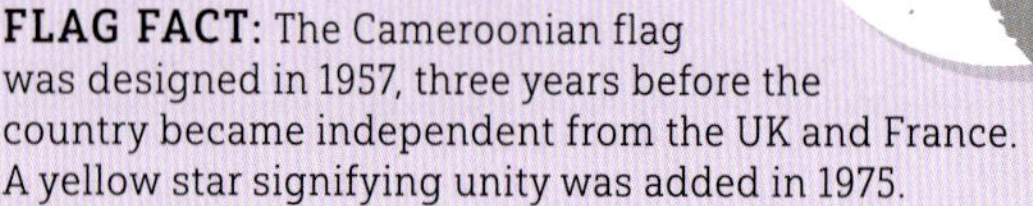

SÃO TOMÉ AND PRÍNCIPE

POPULATION: 223,500

AREA: 372 sq mi (964 sq km)

CURRENCY: Dobra

FLAG ADOPTED: 1975

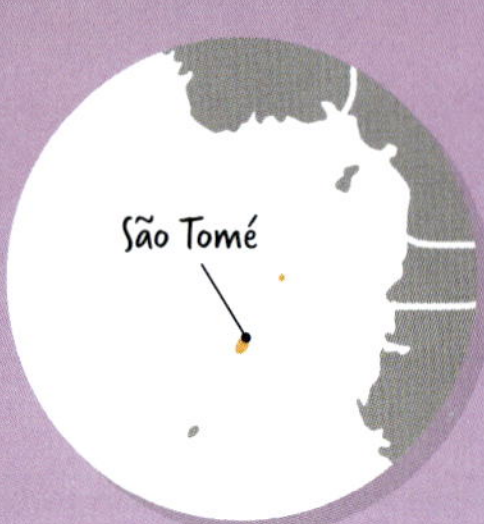

FLAG FACT: The country's flag was adopted in 1975 when São Tomé and Príncipe became independent from Portugal. The two black stars stand for the nation's two main islands and are also a symbol of African pride.

EQUATORIAL GUINEA

POPULATION: 1.8 million

AREA: 10,831 sq mi (28,051 sq km)

CURRENCY: Central African CFA franc

FLAG ADOPTED: 1979

Malabo

FLAG FACT: Today's flag has a coat of arms showing a ceiba tree (the national tree) and the national motto: *Unidad, Paz, Justicia* ("unity, peace, justice"). But in the 1970s, the country's flag briefly displayed a different emblem showing swords, tools, and a cockerel.

CENTRAL AFRICAN REPUBLIC

POPULATION: 5.7 million

AREA: 240,535 sq mi (622,984 sq km)

CURRENCY: Central African CFA franc

FLAG ADOPTED: 1958

Bangui

FLAG FACT: The country's flag features colors associated with both the former colonial power, France (blue and white), and the Pan-African Movement (green and yellow). The red symbolizes a union between the two, while the yellow star stands for independence.

GABON

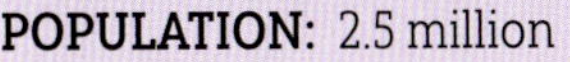

POPULATION: 2.5 million

AREA: 103,346 sq mi (267,667 sq km)

CURRENCY: Central African CFA franc

FLAG ADOPTED: 1960

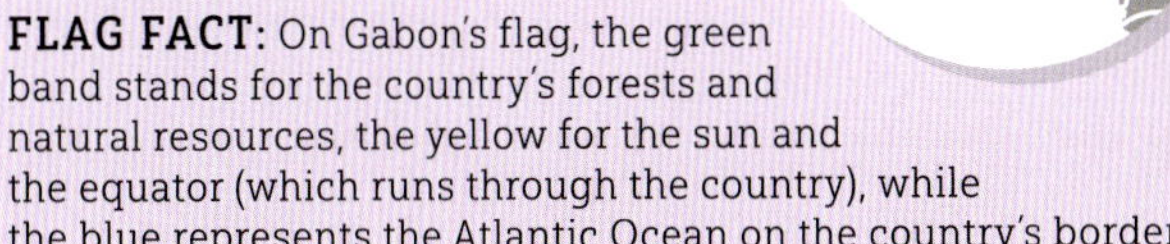

FLAG FACT: On Gabon's flag, the green band stands for the country's forests and natural resources, the yellow for the sun and the equator (which runs through the country), while the blue represents the Atlantic Ocean on the country's border.

REPUBLIC OF THE CONGO

POPULATION: 6.1 million

AREA: 132,047 sq mi (342,000 sq km)

CURRENCY: Central African CFA franc

FLAG ADOPTED: 1959

FLAG FACT: The country's current flag, showing the Pan-African colors (see p.53), was flown from 1959–69 and again from 1991. In between, the country was a communist state with a flag modeled on that of the Soviet Union.

The Soviet Union was a communist state of 15 countries, the largest and most powerful of which was Russia. It had close relationships with many other communist countries, including several in Africa. The union lasted from 1922–91, when it collapsed and its countries became independent. Its flag showed a hammer and sickle, representing the union of agricultural and industrial workers.

DEMOCRATIC REPUBLIC OF THE CONGO

POPULATION: 115 million

AREA: 905,355 sq mi (2,344,858 sq km)

CURRENCY: Congolese franc

FLAG ADOPTED: 2006
(original design 1963)

FLAG FACT: From 1971–97, this country was known as Zaire and had a green flag featuring a hand holding a flaming torch.

ERITREA

POPULATION: 6.3 million
AREA: 45,406 sq mi (117,600 sq km)
CURRENCY: Eritrean nakfa
FLAG ADOPTED: 1995

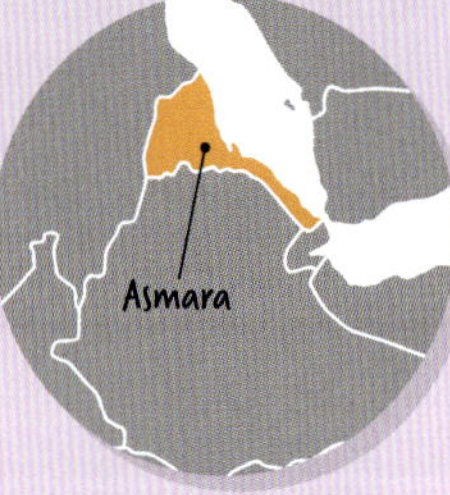

FLAG FACT: The 30 leaves of the olive branch and wreath on the flag represent the 30-year-long war that led to Eritrea gaining independence from Ethiopia.

DJIBOUTI

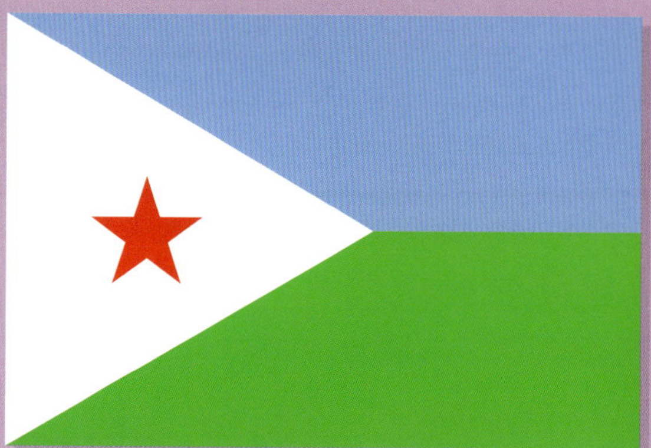

POPULATION: 995,000
AREA: 8,958 sq mi (23,200 sq km)
CURRENCY: Djiboutian franc
FLAG ADOPTED: 1977

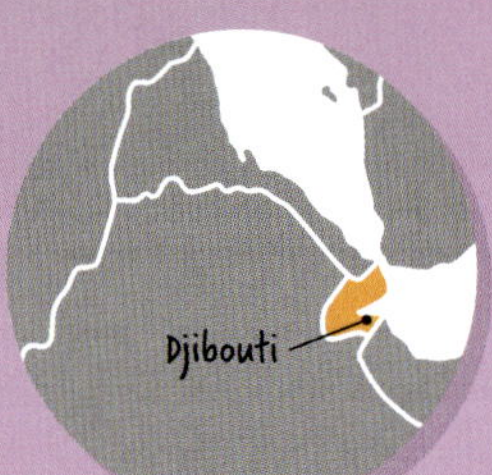

FLAG FACT: The white triangle symbolizes peace, the red star stands for unity, and the other shapes represent the two biggest groups of people in Djibouti—the Issa people (blue) and the Afar people (green).

ETHIOPIA

POPULATION: 119 million
AREA: 426,372.61 sq mi (1,104,300 sq km)
CURRENCY: Ethiopian birr
FLAG ADOPTED: 1996

FLAG FACT: Green, yellow, and red are the traditional colors of Ethiopia. Today, along with black, these colors are known as "Pan-African" colors. They represent African heritage and form the basis of many other flags on the continent (see p.53).

SOMALIA

POPULATION: 13 million
AREA: 246,199 sq mi (637,657 sq km)
CURRENCY: Somali shilling
FLAG ADOPTED: 1954

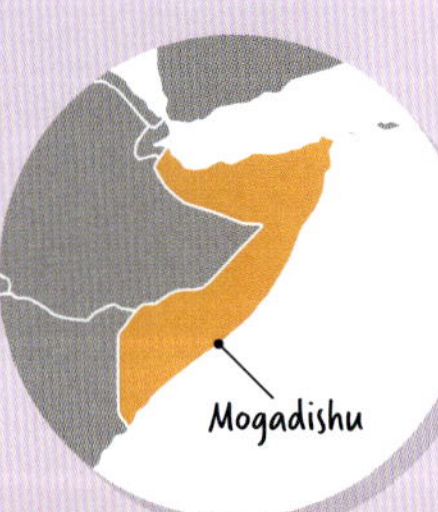

FLAG FACT: The five points of the white star on the flag represent the five areas in Africa where the Somali people have traditionally lived.

UGANDA

POPULATION: 49 million

AREA: 93,065 sq mi (241,038 sq km)

CURRENCY: Ugandan shilling

FLAG ADOPTED: 1962

FLAG FACT: A crested crane sits in the center of Uganda's flag. These beautiful birds are a national symbol and a common sight in Uganda's lush wetlands.

KENYA

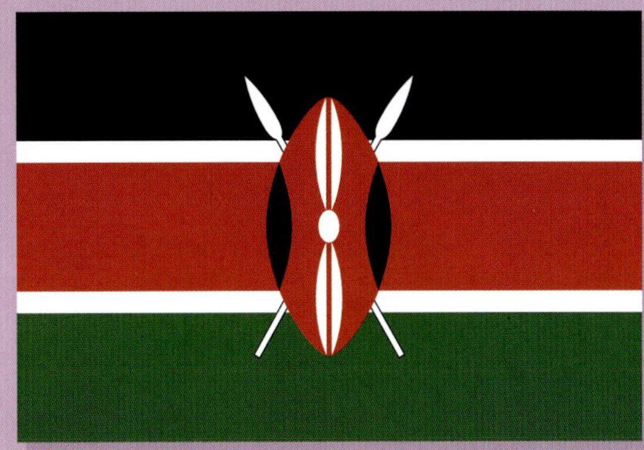

POPULATION: 58 million

AREA: 224,081 sq mi (580,367 sq km)

CURRENCY: Kenyan shilling

FLAG ADOPTED: 1963

FLAG FACT: Kenya's flag features a traditional African shield in the middle. The style and pattern are based on shields used by the Maasai people, who live in Kenya and Tanzania.

RWANDA

POPULATION: 13.6 million

AREA: 10,169 sq mi (26,338 sq km)

CURRENCY: Rwandan franc

FLAG ADOPTED: 2001

FLAG FACT: Rwanda's new flag was adopted in 2001 after a long period of war and unrest. It promotes messages of peace. Sky blue represents hope, yellow represents mineral wealth, green represents the country's rainforests, and the sun at the top right symbolizes unity.

BURUNDI

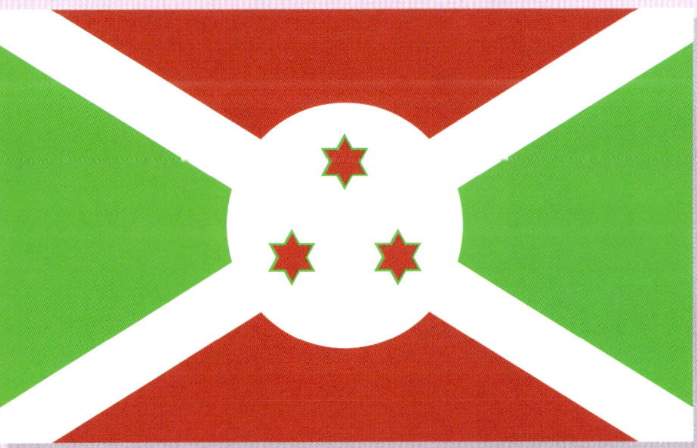

POPULATION: 13.5 million

AREA: 10,750 sq mi (27,830 sq km)

CURRENCY: Burundian franc

FLAG ADOPTED: 1967

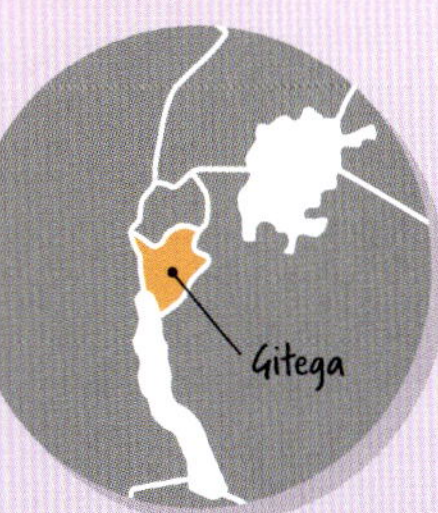

FLAG FACT: The three stars in the middle of Burundi's flag represent the three words of the country's national motto: "Unity, work, progress." They also stand for the three main groups of people who live there—the Tutsi, the Hutu, and the Twa.

TANZANIA

POPULATION: 67 million
AREA: 365,755 sq mi (947,300 sq km)
CURRENCY: Tanzanian shilling
FLAG ADOPTED: 1964

Dodoma

FLAG FACT: In 1964, the countries of Tanganyika and Zanzibar united to become the new country of Tanzania. The flag represents this union, combining the colors of both previous flags.

MOZAMBIQUE

POPULATION: 33 million
AREA: 308,641 sq mi (799,380 sq km)
CURRENCY: Mozambican metical
FLAG ADOPTED: 1983

Maputo

FLAG FACT: Mozambique's flag is one of only two national flags in the world to feature a firearm (the other is Guatemala; see p.17). The weapon symbolizes the country's defense, the hoe stands for its farming communities, and the open book represents education.

MALAWI

POPULATION: 22 million
AREA: 45,747 sq mi (118,484 sq km)
CURRENCY: Malawian kwacha
FLAG ADOPTED: 1964
(readopted in 2012)

Lilongwe

FLAG FACT: Malawi's name means "flaming waters," a reference to the sun setting over Lake Nyasa (also known as Lake Malawi). The half sun on the country's flag represents this, as well as hope for the country's future.

ZAMBIA

POPULATION: 21 million
AREA: 290,585 sq mi (752,618 sq km)
CURRENCY: Zambian kwacha
FLAG ADOPTED: 1964

Lusaka

FLAG FACT: Zambia's flag has an unusual design, with the symbols sitting at the "fly" side, farthest away from the flagpole. One of these symbols is a fish eagle, which is the national bird of Zambia.

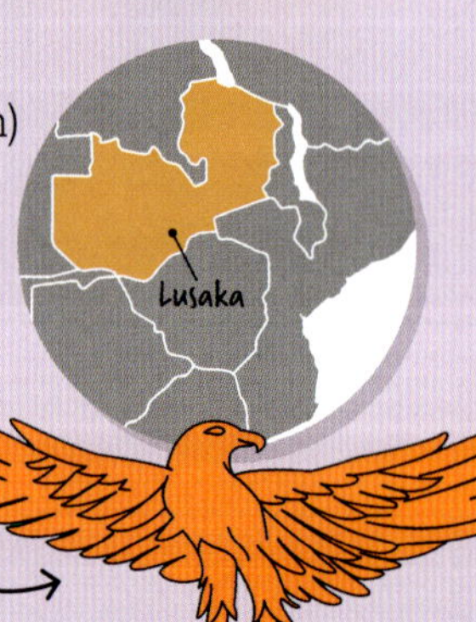

ANGOLA

POPULATION: 37 million

AREA: 481,351 sq mi (1,246,700 sq km)

CURRENCY: Angolan kwanza

FLAG ADOPTED: 1975

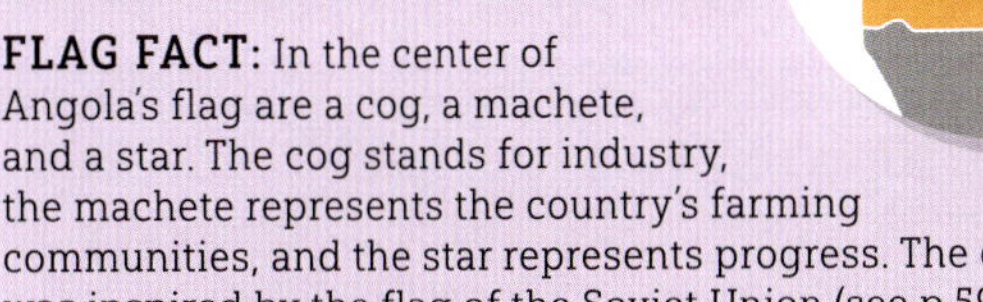

FLAG FACT: In the center of Angola's flag are a cog, a machete, and a star. The cog stands for industry, the machete represents the country's farming communities, and the star represents progress. The design was inspired by the flag of the Soviet Union (see p.59).

NAMIBIA

POPULATION: 2.8 million

AREA: 318,261 sq mi (824,292 sq km)

CURRENCY: Namibian dollar

FLAG ADOPTED: 1990

FLAG FACT: The colors on Namibia's flag represent the country's heroic people (red), peace (white), agriculture (green), and its sky and waters (blue). The golden sun in the top left corner symbolizes life and energy.

BOTSWANA

POPULATION: 2.4 million

AREA: 224,607 sq mi (581,730 sq km)

CURRENCY: Botswanan pula

FLAG ADOPTED: 1966

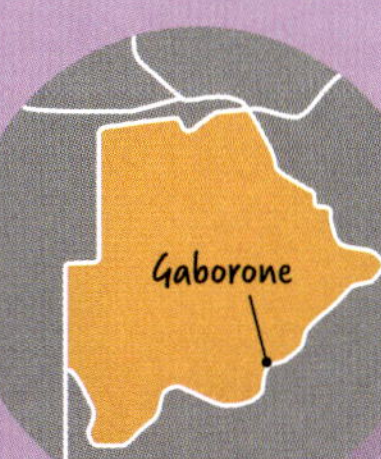

FLAG FACT: The black and white stripes across the middle of Botswana's flag stand for racial harmony. They also recall the stripes of a zebra, which is the country's national animal.

ZIMBABWE

POPULATION: 17 million

AREA: 150,872 sq mi (390,757 sq km)

CURRENCY: Zimbabwe gold

FLAG ADOPTED: 1980

FLAG FACT: Zimbabwe's flag features an image of a mythical bird. The design is based on real-life sculptures of birds that were found in the ruins of the medieval city of Great Zimbabwe.

SOUTH AFRICA

POPULATION: 60 million
AREA: 470,693 sq mi (1,219,090 sq km)
CURRENCY: South African rand
FLAG ADOPTED: 1994

Pretoria
Bloemfontein
Cape Town

FLAG FACT: This is one of the most colorful international flags, with a distinctive Y-shaped pattern of black, gold, green, white, red, and blue. It was designed to coincide with the country's first truly democratic elections in 1994, when all people—of all races—were allowed to take part.

ESWATINI

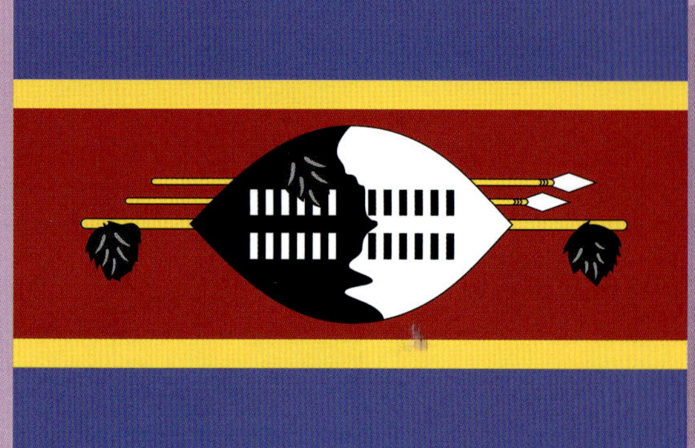

POPULATION: 1.1 million
AREA: 6,704 sq mi (17,364 sq km)
CURRENCY: Swazi lilangeni
FLAG ADOPTED: 1968

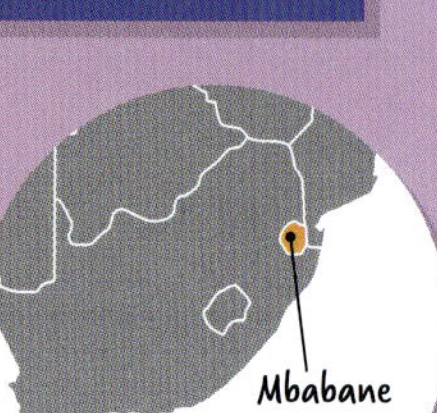

FLAG FACT: The flag depicts a shield, two spears, and a fighting stick of the country's Swazi people. The colors stand for peace (blue), mineral wealth (yellow), and past struggles (red).

LESOTHO

POPULATION: 2.2 million
AREA: 11,720 sq mi (30,355 sq km)
CURRENCY: Lesotho loti
FLAG ADOPTED: 2006

Maseru

FLAG FACT: Lesotho is a high, mountainous country nicknamed "the kingdom in the sky." On its flag, the blue represents the sky, the green the land, and the white, peace. The black shape at the center is a *mokorotlo*, a traditional straw hat.

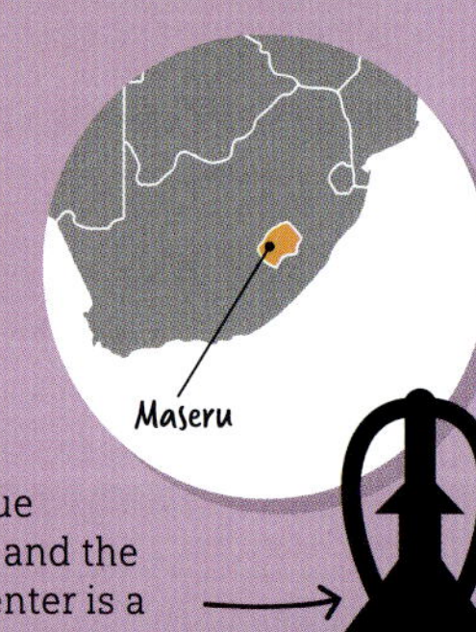

MADAGASCAR

POPULATION: 29 million
AREA: 226,658 sq mi (587,041 sq km)
CURRENCY: Malagasy ariary
FLAG ADOPTED: 1958

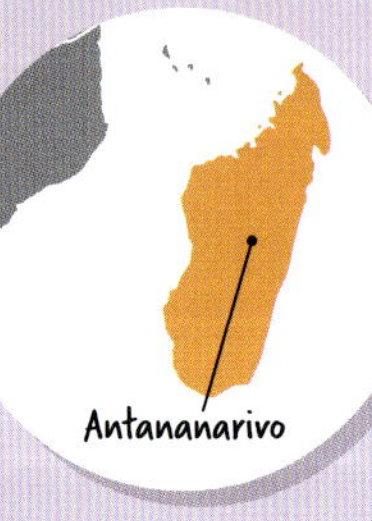

FLAG FACT: The red and white stand for the Merina Kingdom, the forerunner to Madagascar, which France took over in the 19th century. The green stands for the Hova, the common population of the island who became independent from French rule in the mid-20th century.

SEYCHELLES

POPULATION: 98,200
AREA: 176 sq mi (455 sq km)
CURRENCY: Seychellois rupee
FLAG ADOPTED: 1996

FLAG FACT: All the colors on this brightly patterned flag have a meaning: land (green), harmony (white), hard work (red), the sun (yellow), and the sky (blue).

Flag from 1976–77

Flag from 1977–96

COMOROS

POPULATION: 900,100
AREA: 863 sq mi (2,235 sq km)
CURRENCY: Comorian franc
FLAG ADOPTED: 2001

FLAG FACT: The four stars on the Comoros flag stand for the archipelago's four main islands—though one of those islands, Mayotte, is actually administered by France. The crescent moon is a symbol of Islam, the official religion.

MAURITIUS

POPULATION: 1.3 million
AREA: 790 sq mi (2,040 sq km)
CURRENCY: Mauritian rupee
FLAG ADOPTED: 1968

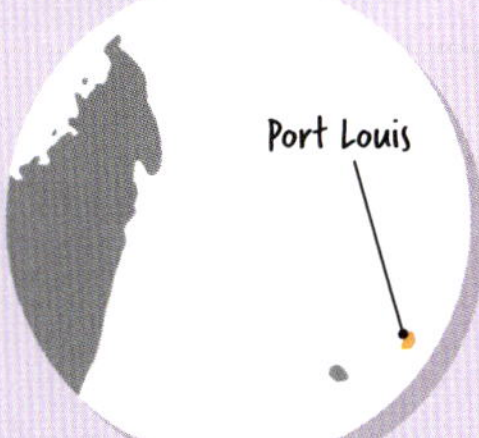

FLAG FACT: Known as the Quatre Bandes ("four bands"), the flag of Mauritius was designed by local schoolteacher Gurudutt Moher. From bottom to top, the colors represent agriculture (green), freedom (yellow), the Indian Ocean (blue), and the struggle for independence (red).

MAPPING THE WORLD'S WILDLIFE

This map shows where some of the world's best-known animals are found in the wild—both on land and at sea. Each type of animal is represented by a number. You can find out what each animal is by locating its number in the key below.

The numbers on the map have colors that correspond to the colors of the continents in the KEY.

KEY

NORTH AMERICA

1. Polar Bear
2. Blue Whale
3. Walrus
4. Bald Eagle
5. Beaver
6. Bison
7. Rattlesnake
8. Alligator
9. Bee Hummingbird
10. Green Turtle

SOUTH AMERICA

11. Poison-Arrow Frog
12. Goliath Birdeater
13. Red-Bellied Piranha
14. Scarlet Macaw
15. Llama
16. Jaguar

EUROPE

17. Red Fox
18. Rabbit
19. Wild Boar

ASIA

20. Beluga Whale
21. Grey Wolf
22. Brown Bear
23. Snow Leopard
24. Panda
25. Giant Hornet
26. Bottle-Nose Dolphin
27. Orangutan
28. Bengal Tiger
29. Komodo Dragon
30. Great Bird of Paradise

AFRICA

31. Camel
32. African Elephant
33. Giraffe
34. Gorilla
35. Cheetah
36. Chameleon
37. Hippopotamus
38. Lion
39. Zebra
40. Great White Shark

AUSTRALIA

41. Kangaroo
42. Clownfish
43. Koala
44. Flying Fox

ANTARCTICA

45. Penguin
46. Orca

MAP THEMES

This is what is known as a thematic map, which means it presents information about a particular theme or topic—in this instance, animals. Thematic maps can be used to show all kinds of information, from different climates to the size of the human population in countries. Thematic maps often use symbols and colors to show information clearly and simply.

Colors have been used on the map to represent the animals' habitats. White is used for snow and ice, green for forests, light orange for grassland, and dark orange for deserts.

In each continent, the numbers are arranged so they go from north to south and from west to east.

ASIA

Everything seems to be bigger in Asia. It's not only the biggest continent, both in terms of area and population, it's also home to the world's largest country by area (Russia), the two largest countries by population (India and China), and the world's biggest, most-populated city, Tokyo, the capital of Japan.

FORESTS AND DESERTS

Asia's landscapes range from the great evergreen forests of the north to the sweltering rainforests of the southeast. It also boasts two of the world's largest deserts, the Arabian Desert of the southwest and the Gobi Desert, where the vast rocky expanses stretch between China and Mongolia.

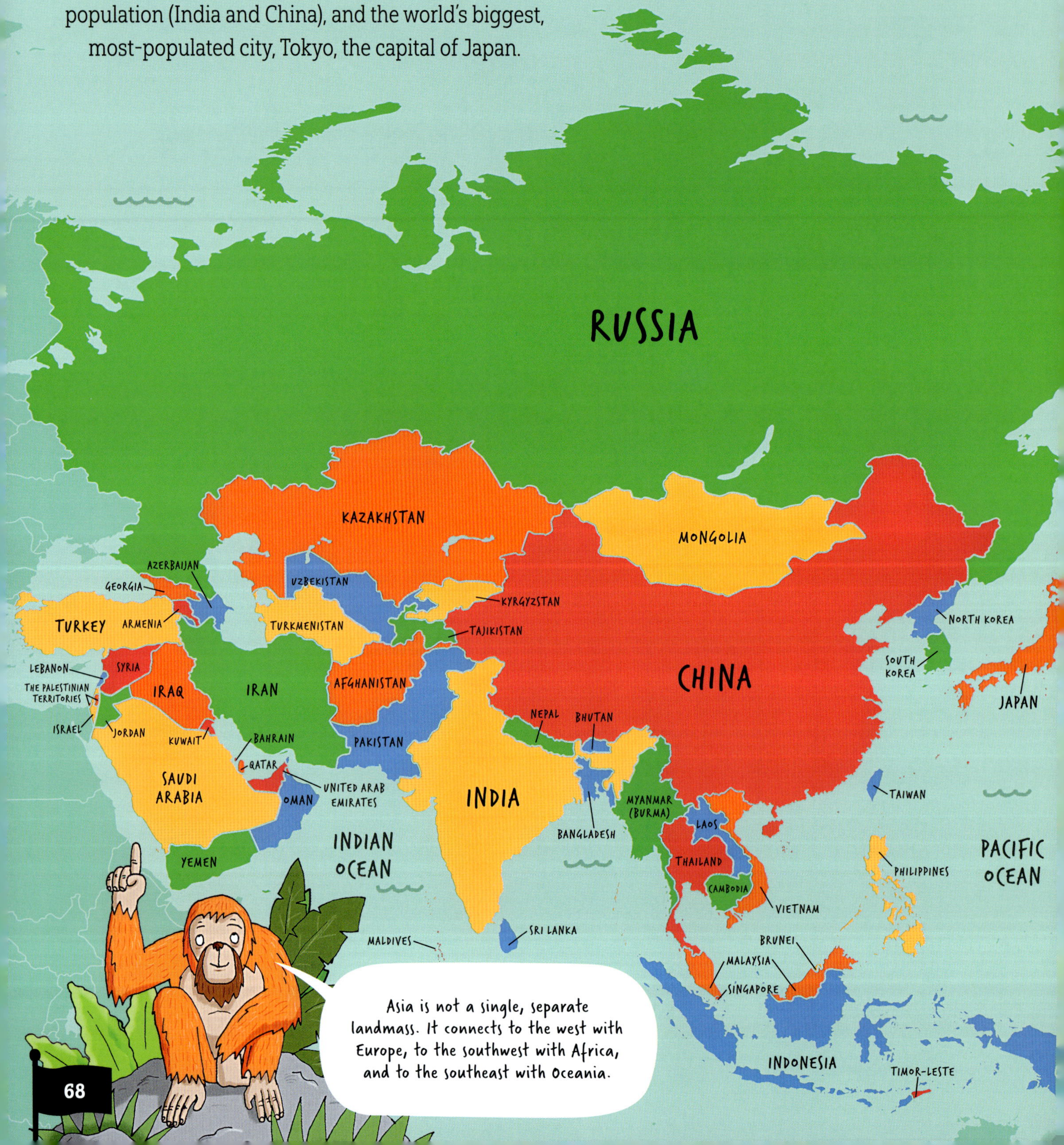

ASIA FACTS

- **SIZE:** 17.2 million sq mi (44.6 million sq km)
- **NO. OF COUNTRIES:** 47
- **POPULATION:** 4.7 billion
- **LARGEST COUNTRY BY AREA:** Russia (also partly in Europe)
- **LARGEST COUNTRY BY AREA WHOLLY IN ASIA:** China
- **LARGEST COUNTRY BY POPULATION:** India
- **SMALLEST COUNTRY BY AREA AND POPULATION:** Maldives
- **LARGEST CITY:** Tokyo (40.8 million people)

WATER WORLD

It's not just the countries that are oversized in Asia. It also boasts the world's largest saltwater lake (the Caspian Sea) and its largest freshwater lake, Lake Baikal in Russia. Baikal is also the world's deepest lake, descending down to 5,387 ft (1,642 m)—that's more than four Empire State Buildings. It contains around a quarter of all the world's non-frozen fresh water.

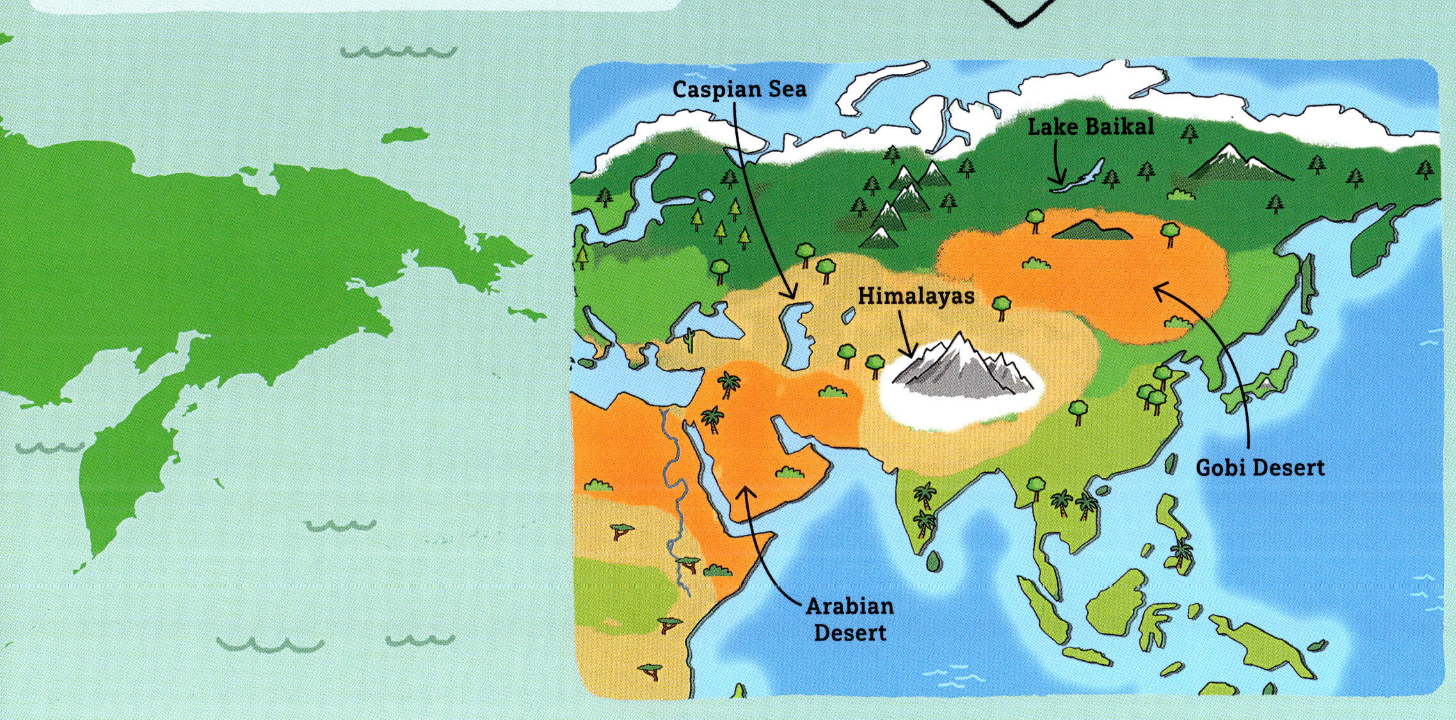

The top 100 tallest mountains on Earth are all found in Asia. The very tallest form the Himalayas, a great arc of towering peaks in Central Asia. Its highest summit—and the highest point on the surface of Earth—is Mount Everest, which is 29,000 ft (8,849 m) high—nearly 20 Empire State Buildings in height.

TURKEY

POPULATION: 84 million

AREA: 302,535 sq mi (783,562 sq km)

CURRENCY: Turkish lira

FLAG ADOPTED: 1936

FLAG FACT: The white crescent moon and star on Turkey's flag are symbols of Islam, the main religion of the country. The flag is otherwise bright red and is often known as Al Bayrak ("the red flag") by Turkish people.

ARMENIA

POPULATION: 3 million

AREA: 11,484 sq mi (29,743 sq km)

CURRENCY: Armenian dram

FLAG ADOPTED: 1990

FLAG FACT: There are various interpretations of the colors on Armenia's flag. One of the most popular is that red stands for the blood shed by Armenians in the past, the blue for the country's skies, and the orange for the land and the people who farm it.

AZERBAIJAN

POPULATION: 10.7 million

AREA: 33,400 sq mi (86,600 sq km)

CURRENCY: Azerbaijani manat

FLAG ADOPTED: 1991

FLAG FACT: The blue stripe represents the Turkic people of the region, the red is for the creation of the modern state, and the green is for Islam. The crescent moon and star are also Islamic symbols.

GEORGIA

POPULATION: 4.9 million

AREA: 26,900 sq mi (69,700 sq km)

CURRENCY: Georgian lari

FLAG ADOPTED: 2004

FLAG FACT: Georgia's flag was partially inspired by the flag of a medieval Georgian ruler, Queen Tamara (1184–1213). The red cross is the symbol of St. George, the patron saint of Georgia—and England—whose flag also features a red cross (see p.36).

SYRIA

POPULATION: 24 million

AREA: 72,370 sq mi (187,437 sq km)

CURRENCY: Syrian pound

FLAG ADOPTED: 1930
(readopted in 2024)

FLAG FACT: During the civil war that began in 2011, the opposition adopted a new flag. It was based on one flown against French rule in the 1930s. After the Syrian government was overthrown by the opposition in 2024, it was adopted as the country's new flag.

LEBANON

POPULATION: 5.4 million

AREA: 4,015 sq mi (10,400 sq km)

CURRENCY: Lebanese pound

FLAG ADOPTED: 1943

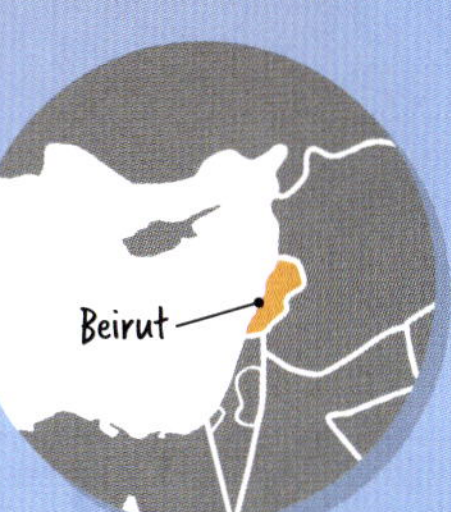

FLAG FACT: In the middle of Lebanon's flag is a picture of a green cedar, the national tree of the country. The white stripe stands for peace, and the red stripes for the blood shed by those who have fought for Lebanese independence.

ISRAEL

POPULATION: 9.4 million

AREA: 8,630 sq mi (21,937 sq km)

CURRENCY: Israeli new shekel

FLAG ADOPTED: 1948

FLAG FACT: The flag is colored blue and white in reference to the traditional prayer shawl of the Jewish people who make up the majority of Israel's population. The six-pointed Star of David in the center is also an ancient Jewish symbol.

THE PALESTINIAN TERRITORIES

POPULATION: 5.3 million

AREA: 2,380 sq mi (6,165 sq km)

CURRENCY: Egyptian pound, Jordanian dinar, & Israeli new shekel

FLAG ADOPTED: 1964

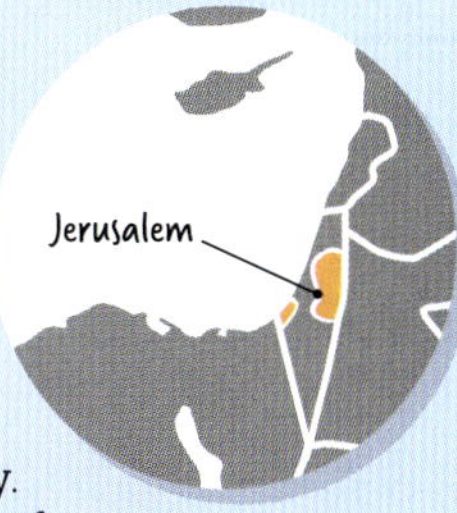

FLAG FACT: Most of the world's countries recognize Palestine as a country. However, around a quarter do not. Its flag of black, white, and green stripes with a red chevron (triangle) represents the Pan-Arab colors (see p.54).

JORDAN

POPULATION: 11.2 million
AREA: 34,495 sq mi (89,342 sq km)
CURRENCY: Jordanian dinar
FLAG ADOPTED: 1928

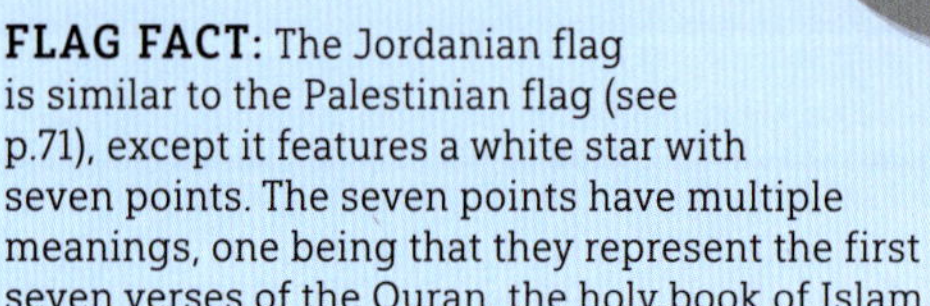

FLAG FACT: The Jordanian flag is similar to the Palestinian flag (see p.71), except it features a white star with seven points. The seven points have multiple meanings, one being that they represent the first seven verses of the Quran, the holy book of Islam.

SAUDI ARABIA

POPULATION: 37 million
AREA: 829,999 sq mi (2,149,690 sq km)
CURRENCY: Saudi riyal
FLAG ADOPTED: 1937

FLAG FACT: The flag features a sword, a symbol of the country's ruling Al Saud family, and the Islamic text: "There is no God but God. Muhammad is the Messenger of God." It has been designed so the text reads right to left, and the sword points left, on both sides.

YEMEN

POPULATION: 32 million
AREA: 203,850 sq mi (527,968 sq km)
CURRENCY: Yemeni rial
FLAG ADOPTED: 1990

FLAG FACT: From the 1960s to 1990, Yemen was divided into two countries: North Yemen and South Yemen. The flag of the united country incorporates the elements that were common to both flags: horizontal stripes in Pan-Arab colors (see p.54).

OMAN

POPULATION: 3.9 million
AREA: 119,500 sq mi (309,500 sq km)
CURRENCY: Omani rial
FLAG ADOPTED: 1970
(slightly adapted in 1995)

FLAG FACT: The country's emblem at the top left of the flag is formed of two crossed swords and a ← J-shaped dagger known as a *khanjar*.

UNITED ARAB EMIRATES

POPULATION: 10 million
AREA: 32,278 sq mi (83,600 sq km)
CURRENCY: UAE dirham
FLAG ADOPTED: 1971

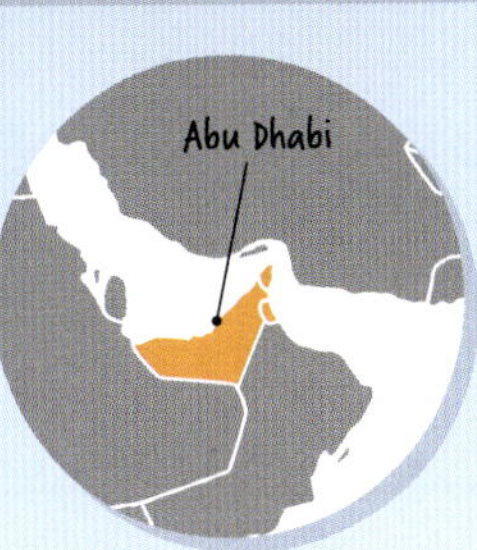

FLAG FACT: When the United Arab Emirates (UAE) became independent from the UK in 1971, the government invited people to send in designs for a new flag. The winning entry—still flown today—was the work of 19-year-old Abdullah Mohammad Al Maainah.

QATAR

POPULATION: 2.6 million
AREA: 4,473 sq mi (11,586 sq km)
CURRENCY: Qatari riyal
FLAG ADOPTED: 1971

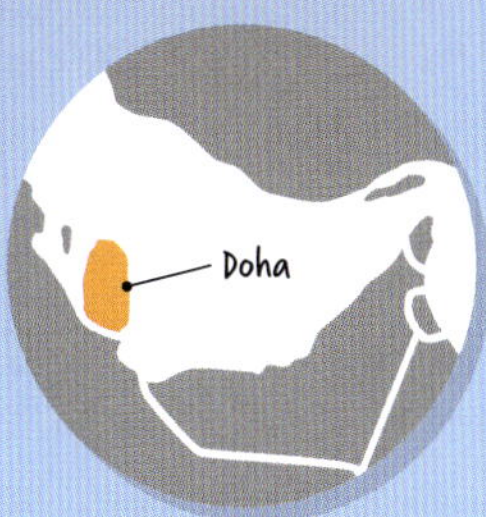

FLAG FACT: Qatar has the only international flag that is more than twice as long as it is high. Its design is similar to that of its neighbor, Bahrain, except it uses a darker shade of red and its white area has nine points (rather than the five on Bahrain's flag).

BAHRAIN

POPULATION: 1.6 million
AREA: 290 sq mi (760 sq km)
CURRENCY: Bahraini dinar
FLAG ADOPTED: 2002

FLAG FACT: Bahrain's flag has gradually changed over the years. In the 1930s, the white area was given a serrated edge with 28 points. These were reduced to eight points in 1972, and then down to five points in 2002 (to represent the five pillars of Islam), creating the current flag.

KUWAIT

POPULATION: 3.1 million
AREA: 6,880 sq mi (17,818 sq km)
CURRENCY: Kuwaiti dinar
FLAG ADOPTED: 1961

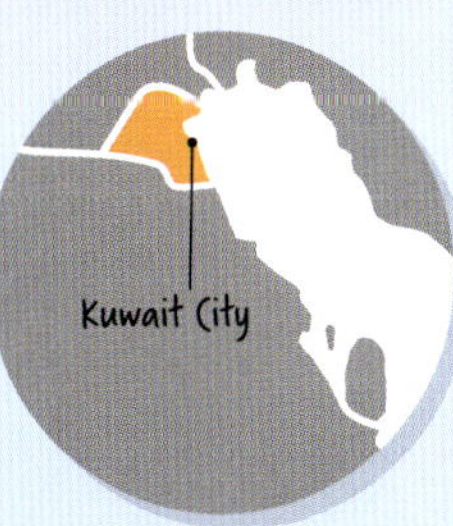

FLAG FACT: Kuwait is the only country to have a trapezium (the black shape) on its flag. Its stripes are in the Pan-Arab colors (see p.54) of green (fertility), white (purity), and red (the blood of the country's enemies).

IRAQ

POPULATION: 42 million

AREA: 169,235 sq mi (438,317 sq km)

CURRENCY: Iraqi dinar

FLAG ADOPTED: 2008

FLAG FACT: Iraq's flag has featured three stripes of red, white, and black since the 1960s, but the green decoration has changed several times. Since 2008, it's shown the Islamic *Takbir*, an Arabic phrase meaning "God is great."

IRAN

POPULATION: 88 million

AREA: 636,372 sq mi (1,648,195 sq km)

CURRENCY: Iranian rial

FLAG ADOPTED: 1980

FLAG FACT: Iran's flag reflects the country's Islamic faith. At the bottom of the green band and at the top of the red band, the words *"Allahu akbar"* ("God is great") are repeated 11 times. The red central emblem also contains Islamic symbols and resembles a tulip flower.

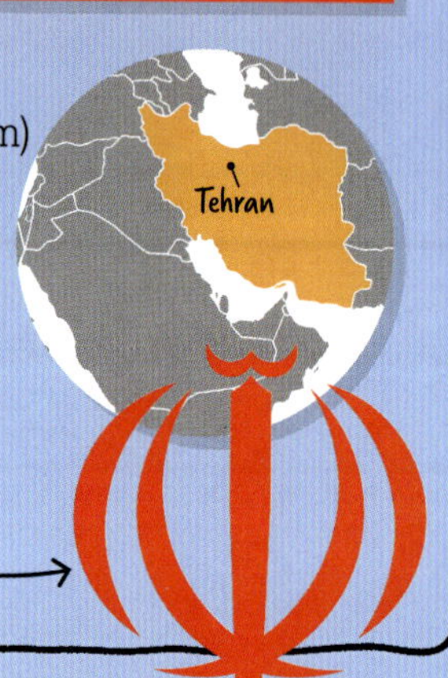

TURKMENISTAN

POPULATION: 5.7 million

AREA: 303,292 sq mi (488,100 sq km)

CURRENCY: Turkmenistani manat

FLAG ADOPTED: 2001

FLAG FACT: The importance of the carpet industry to Turkmenistan is reflected in its flag's vertical red strip, which features five *guls* (designs used in traditional carpets).

UZBEKISTAN

POPULATION: 37 million

AREA: 172,742 sq mi (447,400 sq km)

CURRENCY: Uzbekistani som

FLAG ADOPTED: 1991

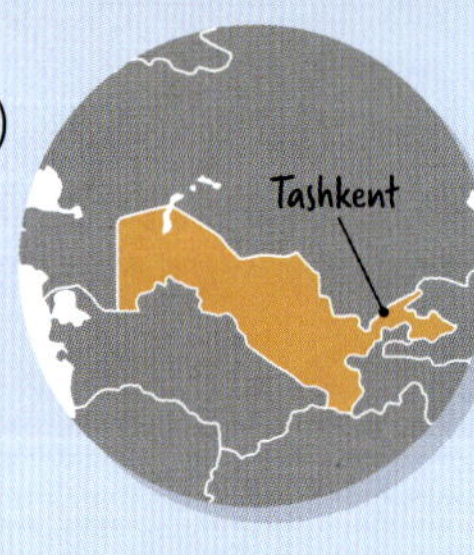

FLAG FACT: Uzbekistan's flag features red fimbriations (narrow borders) between the colored bands. They are said to represent the life force in all living beings. The crescent moon, an Islamic symbol, sits next to 12 stars representing the months of the year.

KAZAKHSTAN

POPULATION: 20 million

AREA: 1,052,100 sq mi (2,724,900 sq km)

CURRENCY: Kazakhstani tenge

FLAG ADOPTED: 1992

Astana

FLAG FACT: On the hoist side of Kazakhstan's flag is an ornamental pattern called *koshkar-muiz* ("the horns of the ram"). The flag also features a sun, representing prosperity, and a steppe eagle, an ancient Kazakh symbol of power and freedom.

KYRGYZSTAN

POPULATION: 6.2 million

AREA: 77,201 sq mi (199,951 sq km)

CURRENCY: Kyrgyzstani som

FLAG ADOPTED: 1992

Bishkek

FLAG FACT: The sun on Kyrgyzstan's flag has 40 rays—one for each of the country's historic tribes. In the middle of the sun is a stylized view of the roof of a yurt, a traditional tent used by the nation's nomadic people.

TAJIKISTAN

POPULATION: 10.4 million

AREA: 56,637 sq mi (144,100 sq km)

CURRENCY: Tajikistani somoni

FLAG ADOPTED: 1992

Dushanbe

FLAG FACT: The colors on the flag represent unity and victory (red), Islam (green), and cotton (white). Cotton farming is an important industry in the country. The crown represents the Tajik people, surrounded by seven stars (seven is considered the number of perfection).

AFGHANISTAN

FLAG ADOPTED: 2002

FLAG ADOPTED: 2021

POPULATION: 40 million

AREA: 251,823 sq mi (652,230 sq km)

CURRENCY: Afghan afghani

Kabul

FLAG FACT: When the Taliban took control of the country in 2021, they adopted a simple white flag with the message: 'There is no God but God. Muhammad is the Messenger of God.' But most countries refuse to acknowledge the Taliban and continue to recognize the country's old red, green and black flag.

INDIA

POPULATION: 1.41 billion
AREA: 1,269,219 sq mi (3,287,263 sq km)
CURRENCY: Indian rupee
FLAG ADOPTED: 1947

FLAG FACT: At the center of the flag is a blue wheel with 24 spokes. This is the Ashoka Chakra, a Buddhist symbol signifying constant movement and progress.

PAKISTAN

POPULATION: 252 million
AREA: 307,374 sq mi (796,095 sq km)
CURRENCY: Pakistani rupee
FLAG ADOPTED: 1947

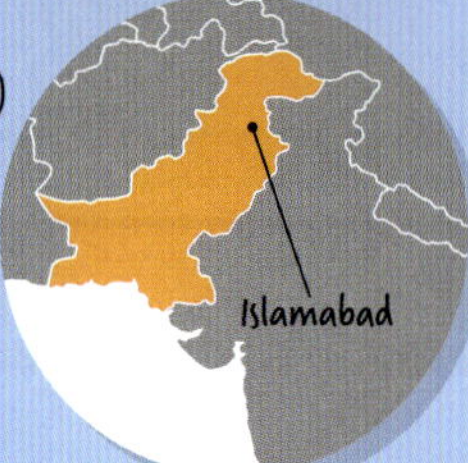

FLAG FACT: Pakistan's flag is colored green with a crescent moon and star—the traditional color and symbols of Islam. On its hoist side is a white stripe, representing the other religions in the country.

NEPAL

POPULATION: 31 million
AREA: 56,827 sq mi (147,181 sq km)
CURRENCY: Nepalese rupee
FLAG ADOPTED: 1962

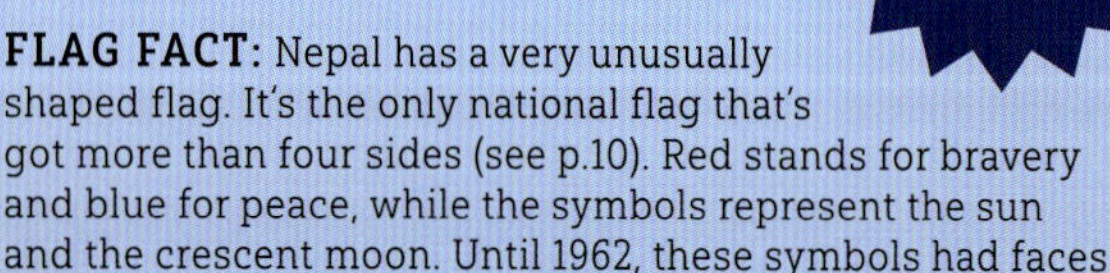

FLAG FACT: Nepal has a very unusually shaped flag. It's the only national flag that's got more than four sides (see p.10). Red stands for bravery and blue for peace, while the symbols represent the sun and the crescent moon. Until 1962, these symbols had faces.

BHUTAN

POPULATION: 885,000
AREA: 14,824 sq mi (38,394 sq km)
CURRENCY: Bhutanese ngultrum
FLAG ADOPTED: 1969

FLAG FACT: The white dragon on Bhutan's flag symbolizes several things. Its color represents peace, its teeth-filled mouth signifies the defense of the country, and the four jewels held in its claws stand for Bhutan's wealth.

BANGLADESH

POPULATION: 169 million

AREA: 57,320 sq mi (148,460 sq km)

CURRENCY: Bangladeshi taka

FLAG ADOPTED: 1972

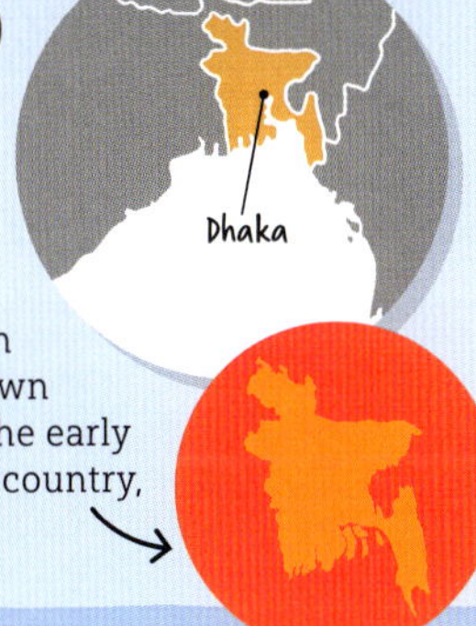

FLAG FACT: The flag has a red circle (representing independence) positioned slightly off-center on a green background (for fertility). When first flown during the independence struggles of the early 1970s, the circle contained a map of the country, which has since been dropped.

SRI LANKA

POPULATION: 22 million

AREA: 25,330 sq mi (65,610 sq km)

CURRENCY: Sri Lankan rupee

FLAG ADOPTED: 1978

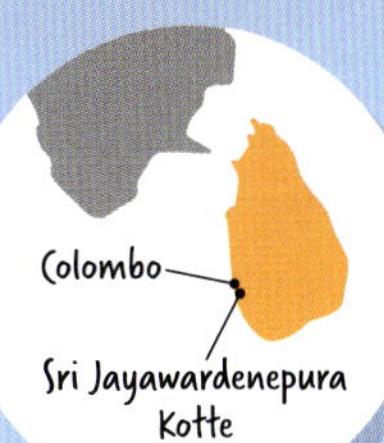

FLAG FACT: The flag's main feature is a gold lion holding a traditional *kastane* sword, a symbol of the country's majority Sinhalese people. The other two main peoples are represented by the orange stripe (Tamils) and the green stripe (Muslims). The lion is framed by four gold leaves from the bo, a tree sacred to Buddhism, the country's largest religion.

MALDIVES

POPULATION: 389,000

AREA: 115 sq mi (298 sq km)

CURRENCY: Maldivian rufiyaa

FLAG ADOPTED: 1965

Malé

FLAG FACT: Made up of over 1,000 islands in the Indian Ocean, with none higher than 7.9 ft (2.4 m) above sea level, this is the world's lowest-lying country. On its flag, red represents struggle, while the white crescent on a green background is a symbol of Islam, the country's main religion.

MYANMAR (BURMA)

POPULATION: 58 million

AREA: 261,228 sq mi (676,578 sq km)

CURRENCY: Myanmar kyat

FLAG ADOPTED: 2010

Nay Pyi Taw

FLAG FACT: The colors stand for purity (white), unity (yellow), fertility (green), and bravery (red). An earlier version of the flag flown from 1974–2010 contained a picture of an ear of rice, the country's staple food.

THAILAND

POPULATION: 70 million

AREA: 198,120 sq mi (513,120 sq km)

CURRENCY: Thai baht

FLAG ADOPTED: 1917

FLAG FACT: The country's previous flag showed a picture of an elephant. It was changed to its current design in 1917 during World War I to make it look more European, as the country had just become an ally to the UK and France in their conflict against Germany.

LAOS

POPULATION: 8 million

AREA: 91,430 sq mi (236,800 sq km)

CURRENCY: Laotian kip

FLAG ADOPTED: 1975

FLAG FACT: The stripes represent struggle (red) and the Mekong River (blue), while the white circle stands for both the moon over the Mekong and unity. The country's previous flag was red with a picture of a white three-headed elephant.

VIETNAM

POPULATION: 106 million

AREA: 127,882 sq mi (331,210 sq km)

CURRENCY: Vietnamese đông

FLAG ADOPTED: 1976
(original design: 1940)

FLAG FACT: From 1955–75, Vietnam was divided into two warring countries. Eventually, North Vietnam won and its flag (above) replaced South Vietnam's version (red stripes on a yellow background) as the reunified country's flag.

CAMBODIA

POPULATION: 17 million

AREA: 69,898 sq mi (181,035 sq km)

CURRENCY: Cambodian riel

FLAG ADOPTED: 1993
(original design: 1848)

FLAG FACT: Cambodia's flag features an image of Angkor Wat, an enormous 12th-century temple complex. This makes Cambodia the only country to feature an image of a building on its flag.

MALAYSIA

POPULATION: 35 million
AREA: 127,355 sq mi (329,847 sq km)
CURRENCY: Malaysian ringgit
FLAG ADOPTED: 1963

FLAG FACT: Known locally as Jalur Gemilang ("stripes of glory"), Malaysia's flag looks a little like the USA's (see p.16). Its 14 stripes (and the 14 points on the star) stand for the country's original states, while the crescent moon is a symbol of the country's main religion, Islam.

BRUNEI

POPULATION: 492,000
AREA: 2,226 sq mi (5,765 sq km)
CURRENCY: Brunei dollar
FLAG ADOPTED: 1959

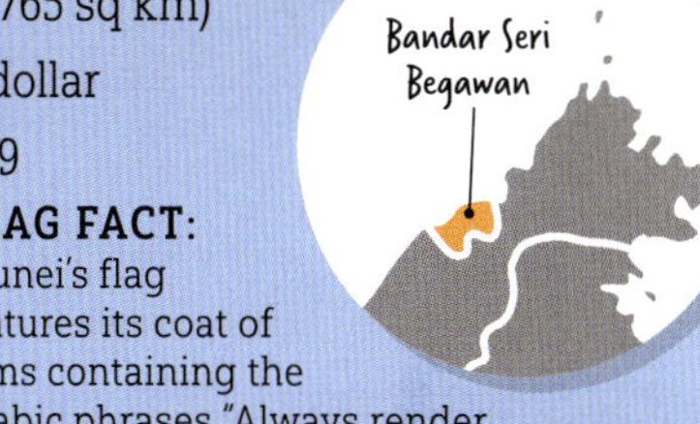

FLAG FACT: Brunei's flag features its coat of arms containing the Arabic phrases "Always render service with God's Guidance" and, below that, "Brunei, abode of peace." The stripes stand for the country's ruler, the sultan (yellow), and its chief ministers (white and black).

SINGAPORE

POPULATION: 6 million
AREA: 278 sq mi (719 sq km)
CURRENCY: Singapore dollar
FLAG ADOPTED: 1959

FLAG FACT: Every part of the Singaporean flag has meaning. The stripes stand for purity (white) and equality (red), while the crescent moon represents the new nation, and the five stars signify the ideals of democracy, peace, progress, justice, and equality.

INDONESIA

POPULATION: 282 million
AREA: 735,358 sq mi (1,904,569 sq km)
CURRENCY: Indonesian rupiah
FLAG ADOPTED: 1945

FLAG FACT: Indonesia's simple flag dates back to the 1200s when it was used by the rulers of the Majapahit Empire, which then controlled parts of Indonesia and Southeast Asia. The flag is very similar to those of Monaco (see p.41) and Poland (see p.40).

TIMOR-LESTE

POPULATION: 1.5 million

AREA: 5,7432 sq mi (14,874 sq km)

CURRENCY: US dollar & East Timor centavo

FLAG ADOPTED: 2002
(original design: 1975)

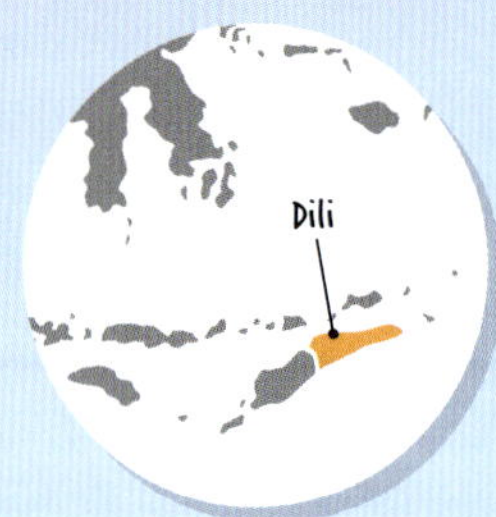

FLAG FACT: The people of Timor-Leste had to fight to free themselves of foreign rule, first by Portugal and then by Indonesia. The flag reflects these struggles, with red standing for spilled blood, yellow for struggle, black for oppression, and the white star for hope.

PHILIPPINES

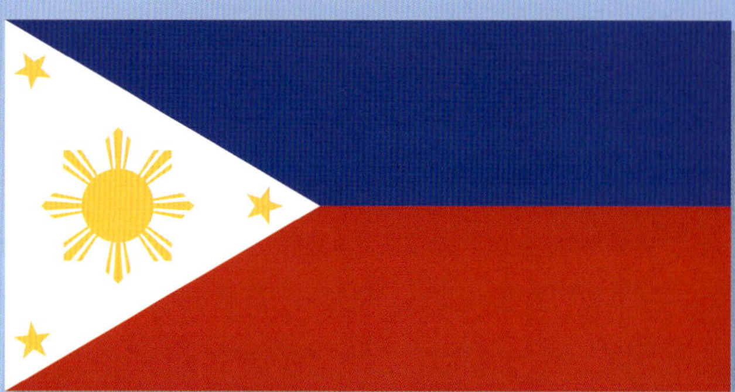

POPULATION: 118 million

AREA: 115,831 sq mi (300,000 sq km)

CURRENCY: Philippine peso

FLAG ADOPTED: 1946
(original design: 1898)

FLAG FACT: The flag was first adopted in 1898 when the country overthrew Spanish rule. It was banned when the USA (and later Japan) took control of the country, but reinstated in 1946 when the country became independent again.

TAIWAN

POPULATION: 24 million

AREA: 13,892 sq mi (35,980 sq km)

CURRENCY: New Taiwan dollar

FLAG ADOPTED: 1945
(original design: 1895)

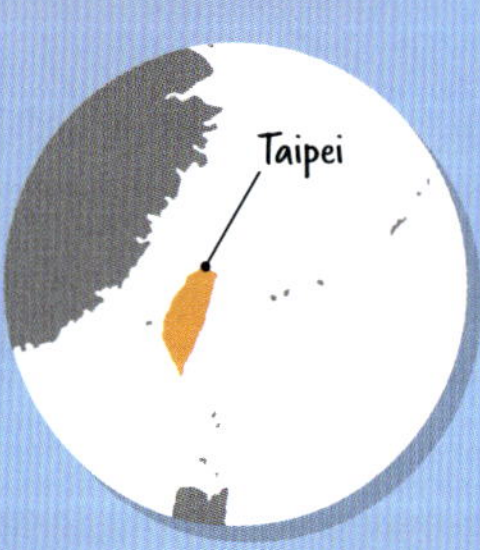

FLAG FACT: Taiwan's status as an independent country is not accepted by China, which believes it should be part of China. As such, its athletes compete in the Olympics using a different flag and a different name: Chinese Taipei.

CHINA

POPULATION: 1.41 billion

AREA: 3,705,410 sq mi (9,596,960 sq km)

CURRENCY: Chinese renminbi

FLAG ADOPTED: 1949

Beijing

FLAG FACT: When China became a communist country in 1949, it introduced a new flag that is mostly red, which is both a traditional Chinese color and associated with communism. The large yellow star stands for China and the four smaller stars for its various peoples.

NORTH KOREA

POPULATION: 26 million

AREA: 46,540 sq mi (120,538 sq km)

CURRENCY: Korean People's won

FLAG ADOPTED: 1948

FLAG FACT: Once a single country, Korea divided into North and South Korea in 1948. The northern part became communist and adopted a red star, a symbol associated with communism, on its flag. The white stripes stand for purity and the blue for peace.

MONGOLIA

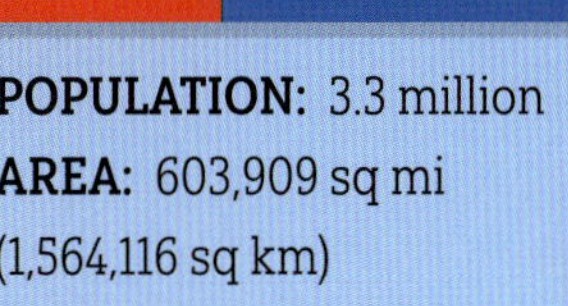

POPULATION: 3.3 million

AREA: 603,909 sq mi (1,564,116 sq km)

CURRENCY: Tögrög

FLAG ADOPTED: 1992

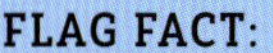

FLAG FACT: Mongolia's flag has two red stripes signifying progress and a blue stripe signifying the sky. On the left is a national symbol, the Soyombo, made up of various yellow shapes, including a flame, sun, moon, and two fish with open eyes signifying vigilance.

SOUTH KOREA

POPULATION: 52 million

AREA: 38,502 sq mi (99,720 sq km)

CURRENCY: Korean Republic won

FLAG ADOPTED: 1948
(original design: 1882)

FLAG FACT: At the flag's center is a circle symbol called a *taegeuk* representing the balance of opposing forces. Surrounding this are four traditional symbols called trigrams representing water (top right), earth (bottom right), fire (bottom left), and the heavens (top left).

JAPAN

POPULATION: 123 million

AREA: 145,914 sq mi (377,915 sq km)

CURRENCY: Japanese yen

FLAG ADOPTED: 1868

FLAG FACT: The flag has a simple design showing a red circle on a white background. The circle represents the sun and reflects the country's historic nickname: "the Land of the Rising Sun." Local people often refer to the flag as Hinomaru ("the ball of the sun").

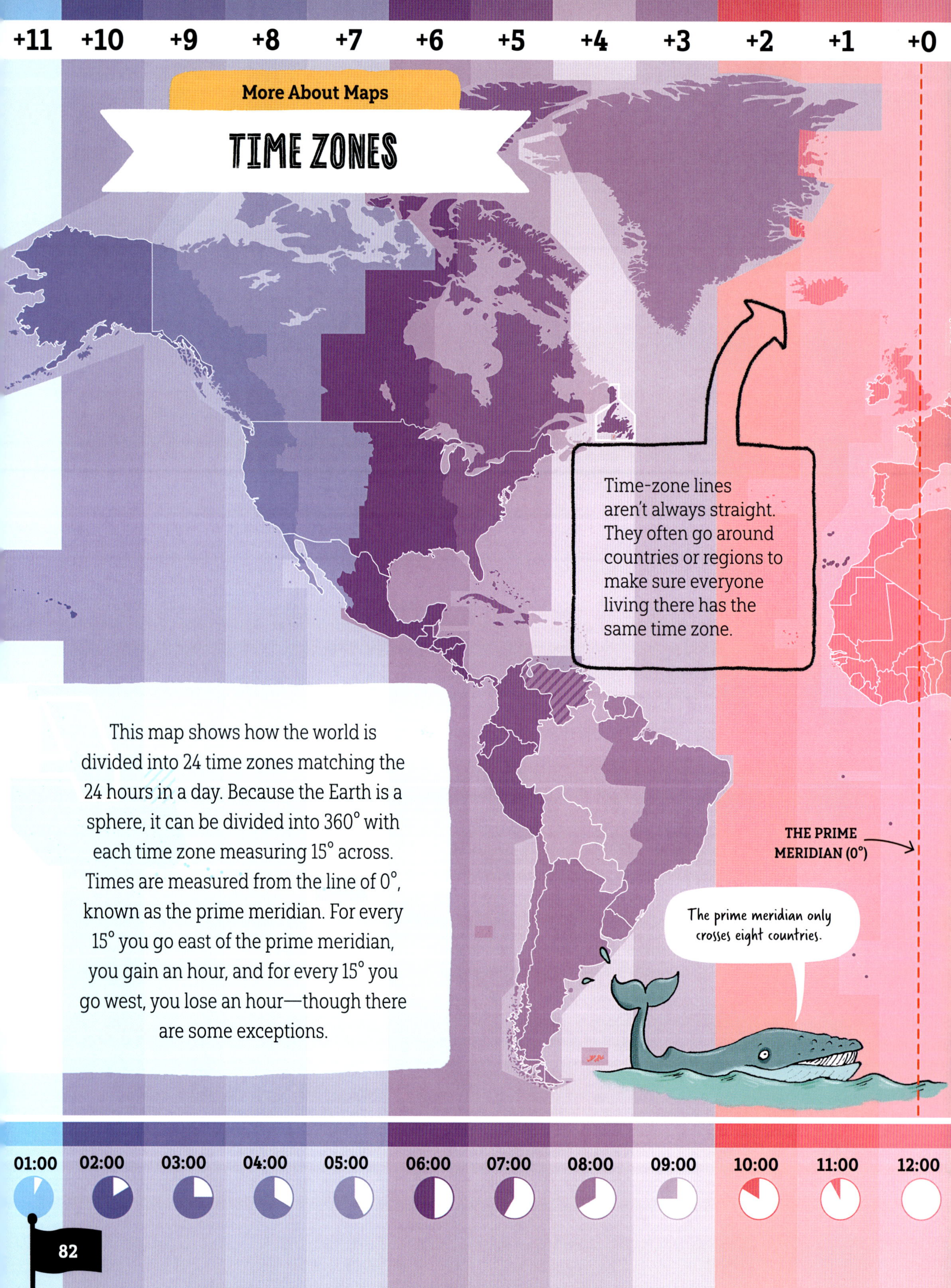
+11
+10
+9
+8
+7
+6
+5
+4
+3
+2
+1
+0
More About Maps
TIME ZONES
Time-zone lines aren't always straight. They often go around countries or regions to make sure everyone living there has the same time zone.
This map shows how the world is divided into 24 time zones matching the 24 hours in a day. Because the Earth is a sphere, it can be divided into 360° with each time zone measuring 15° across. Times are measured from the line of 0°, known as the prime meridian. For every 15° you go east of the prime meridian, you gain an hour, and for every 15° you go west, you lose an hour—though there are some exceptions.
THE PRIME MERIDIAN (0°)
The prime meridian only crosses eight countries.
01:00
02:00
03:00
04:00
05:00
06:00
07:00
08:00
09:00
10:00
11:00
12:00

+2
+3
+4
+5
+6
+7
+8
+9
+10
+11
+12
Russia is the world's largest country and has the greatest number of time zones: 11.
Halfway across the world from the prime meridian is the international date line. This marks the boundary between one day and the next.
Despite being one of the biggest countries in the world, China only recognizes one time zone, so the time there is the same wherever you are.
14:00
15:00
16:00
17:00
18:00
19:00
20:00
21:00
22:00
23:00
24:00

OCEANIA

Australia is the world's smallest continent by area. It lies within a larger area known as Oceania, which includes many other islands stretched out across the Pacific Ocean—sometimes great distances from one another. Other than Antarctica, Oceania is the least-populated continental region, with most of its people living in Australia.

Not all of the islands in Oceania form parts of independent countries. Some are overseas territories of other nations, including Australia, New Zealand, the USA, the UK, and France.

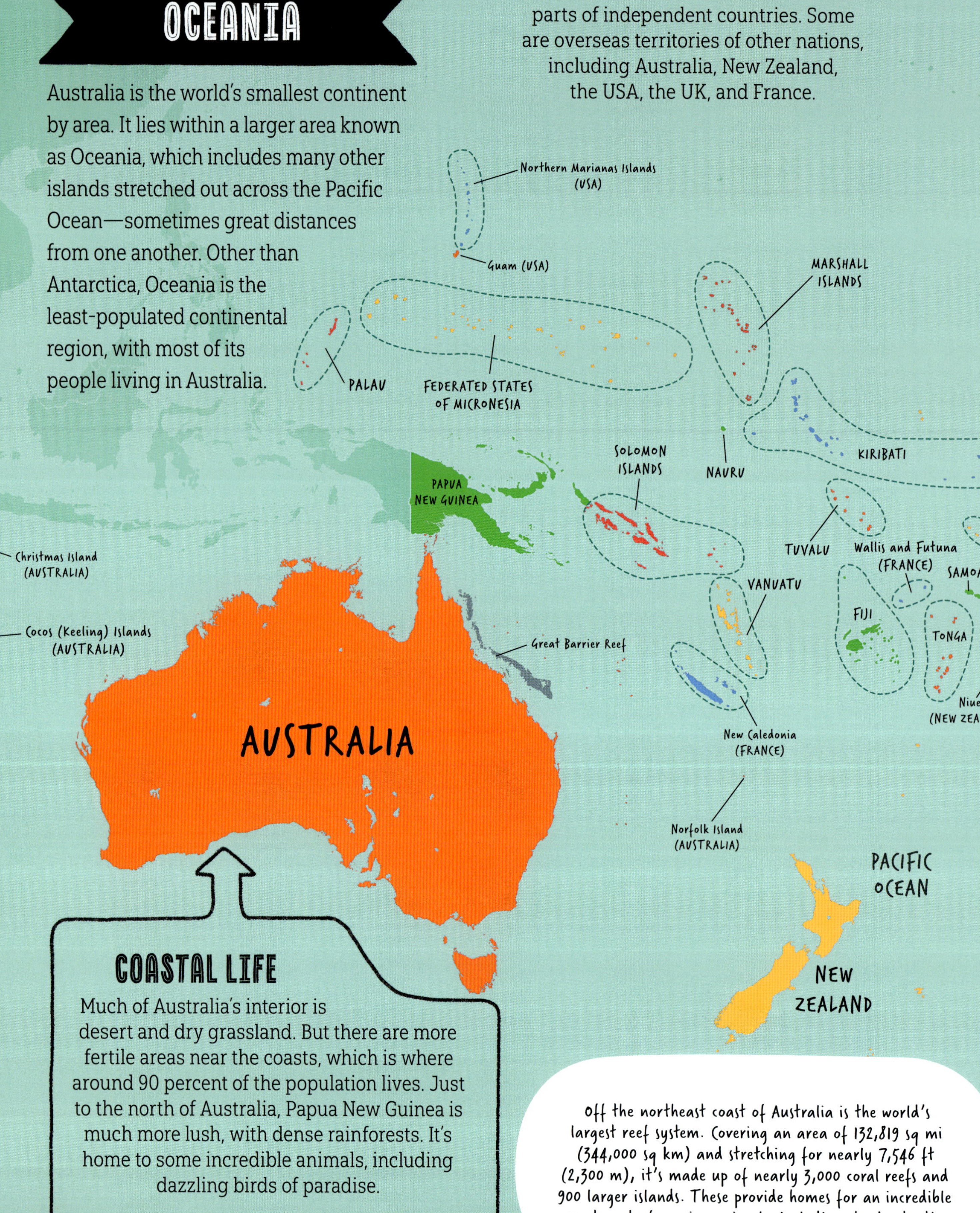

COASTAL LIFE

Much of Australia's interior is desert and dry grassland. But there are more fertile areas near the coasts, which is where around 90 percent of the population lives. Just to the north of Australia, Papua New Guinea is much more lush, with dense rainforests. It's home to some incredible animals, including dazzling birds of paradise.

Off the northeast coast of Australia is the world's largest reef system. Covering an area of 132,819 sq mi (344,000 sq km) and stretching for nearly 7,546 ft (2,300 m), it's made up of nearly 3,000 coral reefs and 900 larger islands. These provide homes for an incredible assortment of marine animals, including sharks, turtles, and brightly colored clownfish, just like me.

STRETCHED OUT

Some of the countries in Oceania are made up of dozens of islands stretched out across the ocean. For instance, Kiribati has 33 islands that stretch for around 2,423 mi (3,900 km) from east to west and across 1.3 million sq mi (3.4 million sq km) of ocean. It is the only country located in all four hemispheres, having islands both above and below the equator and on either side of the international date line (see p.83). Its location means it is the first country in the world to welcome each New Year.

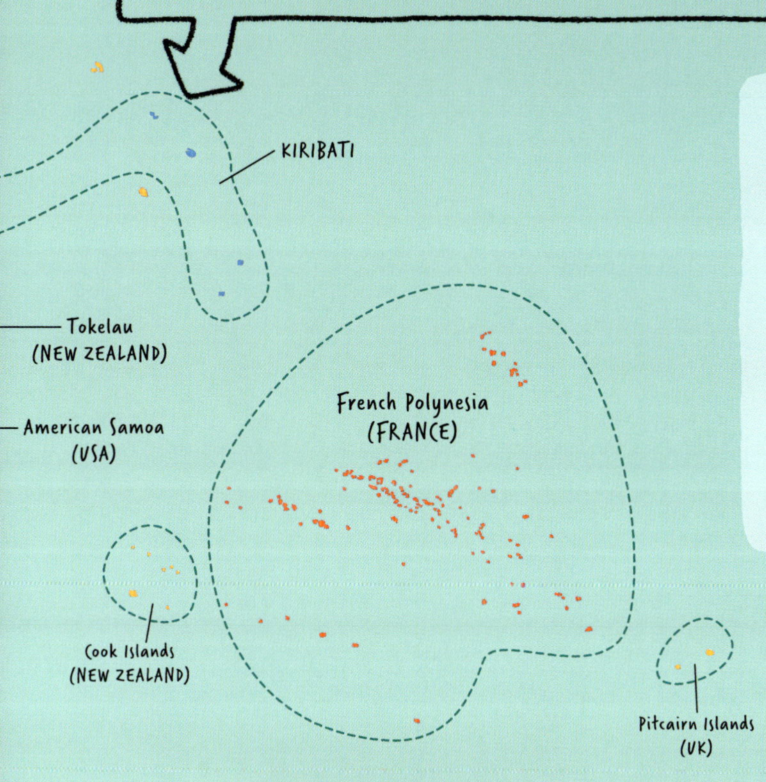

OCEANIA FACTS

- **SIZE:** 3.5 million sq mi (9 million sq km)
- **NO. OF COUNTRIES:** 14
- **POPULATION:** 44 million
- **LARGEST COUNTRY BY AREA AND POPULATION:** Australia
- **SMALLEST COUNTRY BY AREA AND POPULATION:** Tuvalu
- **LARGEST CITY:** Sydney, Australia (5.5 million people)

ISLAND BY ISLAND

Many of the islands in the Pacific lie separated by thousands of miles of ocean. They were gradually settled by people beginning around 5,000 years ago. They used special double-hulled canoes to sail between the islands. New Zealand was the last large landmass on Earth to be inhabited when it was settled by the Māori people from around 1250 CE.

The region of Oceania takes up much of the world's biggest ocean, the Pacific. In fact, the Pacific contains so much water—65 million sq mi (168 million sq km) of it—that it could swallow the largest continent, Asia, over three times. Some animals, such as whales and us green turtles, regularly swim across the entire ocean on the lookout for tasty things to eat.

FEDERATED STATES OF MICRONESIA

POPULATION: 100,000

AREA: 271 sq mi (702 sq km)

CURRENCY: US dollar

FLAG ADOPTED: 1978

Palikir

FLAG FACT: The country consists of over 600 islands divided into four states: Chuuk, Kosrae, Pohnpei, and Yap. Each state is represented on the country's flag by a star. The blue stands for the surrounding ocean.

Flag of Chuuk

Flag of Kosrae

Flag of Pohnpei

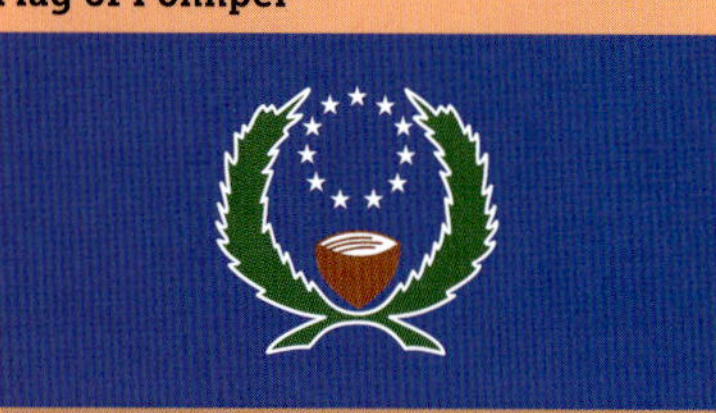

Flag of Yap

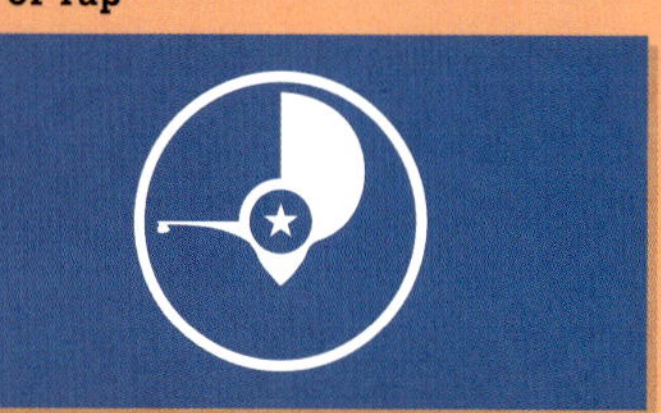

PALAU

POPULATION: 22,000

AREA: 177 sq mi (459 sq km)

CURRENCY: US dollar

FLAG ADOPTED: 1981

Ngerulmud

FLAG FACT: Palau's flag looks a bit like Japan's (see p.81), except with a blue background (representing the Pacific Ocean and independence) and a yellow circle. Unlike on Japan's flag, the circle represents the full moon rather than the sun, and is slightly off-center.

MARSHALL ISLANDS

POPULATION: 82,000

AREA: 70 sq mi (181 sq km)

CURRENCY: US dollar

FLAG ADOPTED: 1979

FLAG FACT: The star on the Marshall Islands' flag has the most points of any star on an international flag: 24. They represent the country's main districts. The diagonal lines stand for the two main island chains: the Ralik ("sunset") chain in orange and the Ratak ("sunrise") chain in white.

KIRIBATI

POPULATION: 117,000
AREA: 313 sq mi (811 sq km)
CURRENCY: Australian dollar
FLAG ADOPTED: 1979

FLAG FACT: Above the sun flies a gold-colored frigate bird, a symbol of power and freedom. The three wavy white lines represent the country's main island groups: the Gilbert, the Phoenix, and the Line Islands.

NAURU

POPULATION: 9,900
AREA: 8 sq mi (21 sq km)
CURRENCY: Australian dollar
FLAG ADOPTED: 1968

FLAG FACT: The flag's design is meant to roughly show the country's geographic location. The white star represents the island, the blue is the surrounding ocean, while the yellow line stands for the equator, which lies just to the north.

SOLOMON ISLANDS

POPULATION: 727,000
AREA: 11,157 sq mi (28,896 sq km)
CURRENCY: Solomon Islands dollar
FLAG ADOPTED: 1977

FLAG FACT: Two other designs were initially chosen to be the country's flag but were eventually dropped in favor of the current one. It represents the five main island groups (white stars), the ocean (blue), the land (green), and sunshine (yellow).

TUVALU

POPULATION: 11,700
AREA: 10 sq mi (26 sq km)
CURRENCY: Tuvaluan dollar
FLAG ADOPTED: 1997
(original design: 1978)

Funafuti

FLAG FACT: Once a British dependency, Tuvalu's flag still features the Union Jack (see p.37). The stars represent the country's nine islands, which are arranged according to their approximate geographic pattern against a blue background representing the ocean.

SAMOA

POPULATION: 209,000
AREA: 1,093 sq mi (2,831 sq km)
CURRENCY: Tālā
FLAG ADOPTED: 1949

FLAG FACT: The colors are the same as the flag of New Zealand, from which Samoa gained independence in 1962. The stars form the shape of the Southern Cross, a Southern Hemisphere constellation that features on several other regional flags.

VANUATU

POPULATION: 318,000
AREA: 4,706 sq mi (12,189 sq km)
CURRENCY: Vatu
FLAG ADOPTED: 1980

FLAG FACT: On the left of the flag is an image of a boar's tusk (a symbol of prosperity) and crossed leaves from the local namale tree (a symbol of peace).

FIJI

POPULATION: 952,000
AREA: 7,056 sq mi (18,274 sq km)
CURRENCY: Fijian dollar
FLAG ADOPTED: 1970

FLAG FACT: The flag retains the British flag (see p.37) in the canton (corner) as a link to the time when Fiji was part of the British Empire. On the right is a shield from the country's coat of arms, showing palm trees, bananas, a dove of peace, and a lion holding a coconut.

TONGA

POPULATION: 105,000
AREA: 288 sq mi (747 sq km)
CURRENCY: Pa'anga
FLAG ADOPTED: 1875

FLAG FACT: Around 97 percent of Tonga's population identify as Christians, and the country's flag features both a Christian symbol (the cross) and a color associated with Christianity (red). The country has passed a law that forbids the design of the flag from being changed.

PAPUA NEW GUINEA

POPULATION: 10 million
AREA: 178,703 sq mi (462,840 sq km)
CURRENCY: Kina
FLAG ADOPTED: 1971

FLAG FACT: This was designed by 15-year-old Susan Karike, who entered a competition in 1971 to design a new national flag. It features the Southern Cross constellation and one of the country's most famous animals, a bird of paradise.

AUSTRALIA

POPULATION: 27 million
AREA: 2,988,902 sq mi (7,741,220 sq km)
CURRENCY: Australian dollar
FLAG ADOPTED: 1908

FLAG FACT: Australia's flag shows the stars of the Southern Cross constellation on the right-hand side and, on the left-hand side, an extra seven-pointed star representing the country's six states and other territories.

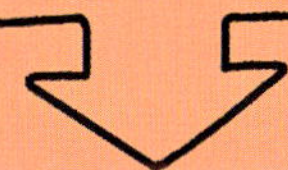

Two other flags are often flown alongside the Australian flag. These represent the Indigenous Peoples who had been living in Australia for many thousands of years before European settlers showed up.

This is the flag of Australia's Aboriginal Peoples, representing the country's soil (the red stripe), its Indigenous Peoples (the black stripe), and the sun (the yellow circle).

This is the flag of the Torres Strait Islanders from an island group north of the mainland. It features a traditional headdress known as a *dhari* around a five-pointed star.

NEW ZEALAND

POPULATION: 5.2 million
AREA: 103,798 sq mi (268,838 sq km)
CURRENCY: New Zealand dollar
FLAG ADOPTED: 1902

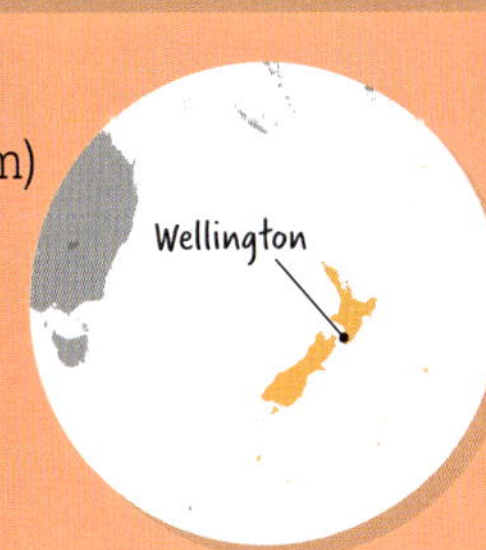

FLAG FACT: In 2015, New Zealand held a referendum (national vote) on whether to change its flag from one featuring the Southern Cross and the flag of the UK (see p.37) to one showing a silver fern, a modern symbol of New Zealand. The people voted to retain the old flag.

ALL TYPES OF MAPS

Maps can be used to show lots of different types of information—from what the weather will be like tomorrow and the heights of hills to how many people there are in the world and even fictional places in a novel or game. Maps are often made using certain conventions (traditional ways of doing things). Sometimes, tweaking these conventions allows us to look at the world in a whole new way.

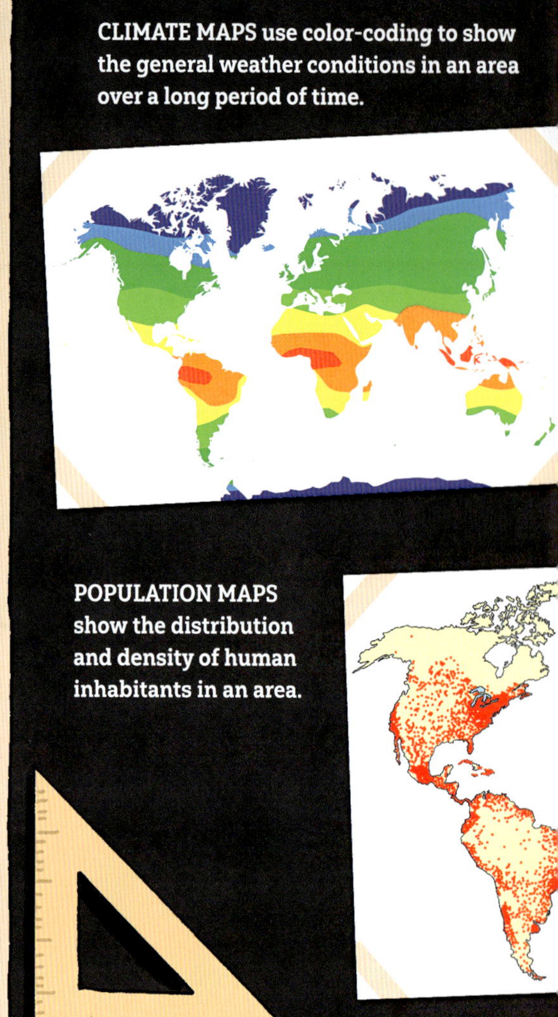

CLIMATE MAPS use color-coding to show the general weather conditions in an area over a long period of time.

POPULATION MAPS show the distribution and density of human inhabitants in an area.

UPTURNING CONVENTIONS

One common mapmaking convention is to place Europe at the center of a world map. This is mainly because the first maps of the entire world were produced in Europe. Another common modern convention is to place north at the top of the map, but this wasn't always the case. Many early maps had east at the top, as that is where the sun rises.

This map places Australia, not Europe, at the center of the world. It's also "upside down," with south at the top and north at the bottom.

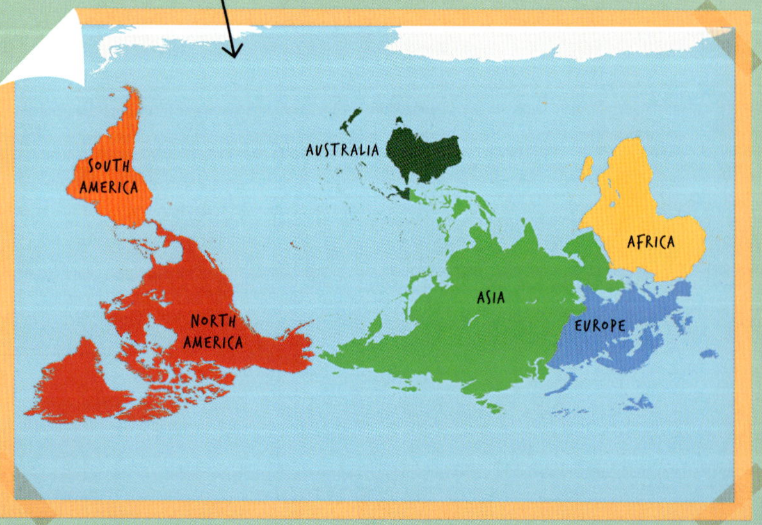

The "upside-down" map isn't wrong. It just looks a bit strange to us because it's not following familiar conventions. Having conventions helps us to understand maps as it means we all read them in the same way.

WEATHER MAPS use symbols and colors to show weather conditions in the near future.

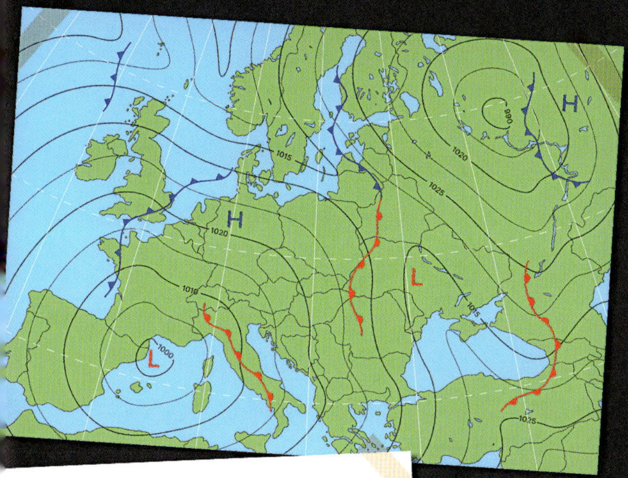

TOPOGRAPHIC MAPS use symbols known as contour lines to show areas of different height.

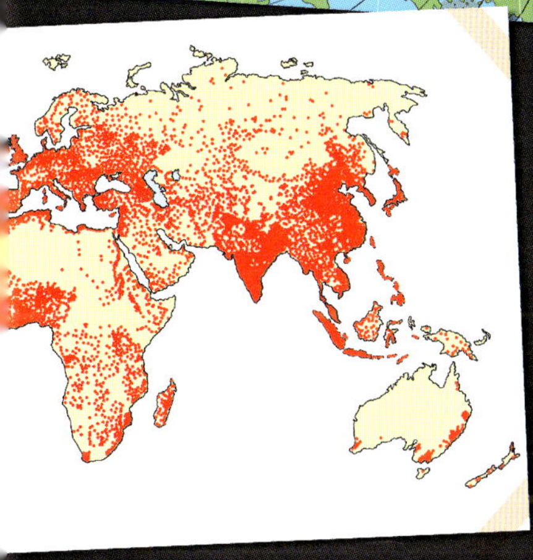

FICTIONAL MAPS are often used in novels and video games to bring the make-believe worlds to life.

There are many different types of maps, all of which use their own conventions to show different information. Some of the most common types are shown above.

OVERSEAS TERRITORIES

Most of the world's land is divided up into countries. But some areas aren't countries in their own right. They are territories that belong to other countries. Many have been highlighted on the maps in this book. Some other areas are disputed, which means there's no international agreement about who owns the land. The world's largest area of disputed land is Antarctica. Seven countries claim ownership of parts of the continent, but none agree with the others' claims.

END OF EMPIRES

Some territories belong to countries that are far away from them, often in another continent. This is usually because the territory was once part of an empire, such as those built up by several European countries in centuries past, including the UK, France, and the Netherlands. In more recent times, these empires have been disbanded and most of the territories became independent. However, some (usually small) territories have remained under the control of the parent country.

ANTARCTICA

On a conventional flat map of the world, such as the one on pages 12–13, Antarctica looks like a long area of land stretched out across the bottom of the map. But when seen from above, Antarctica is actually a roughly circular-shaped continent. This map shows both the shape of Antarctica, the claims on its territory made by various countries (several of which overlap), and the proposed flags for these territories.

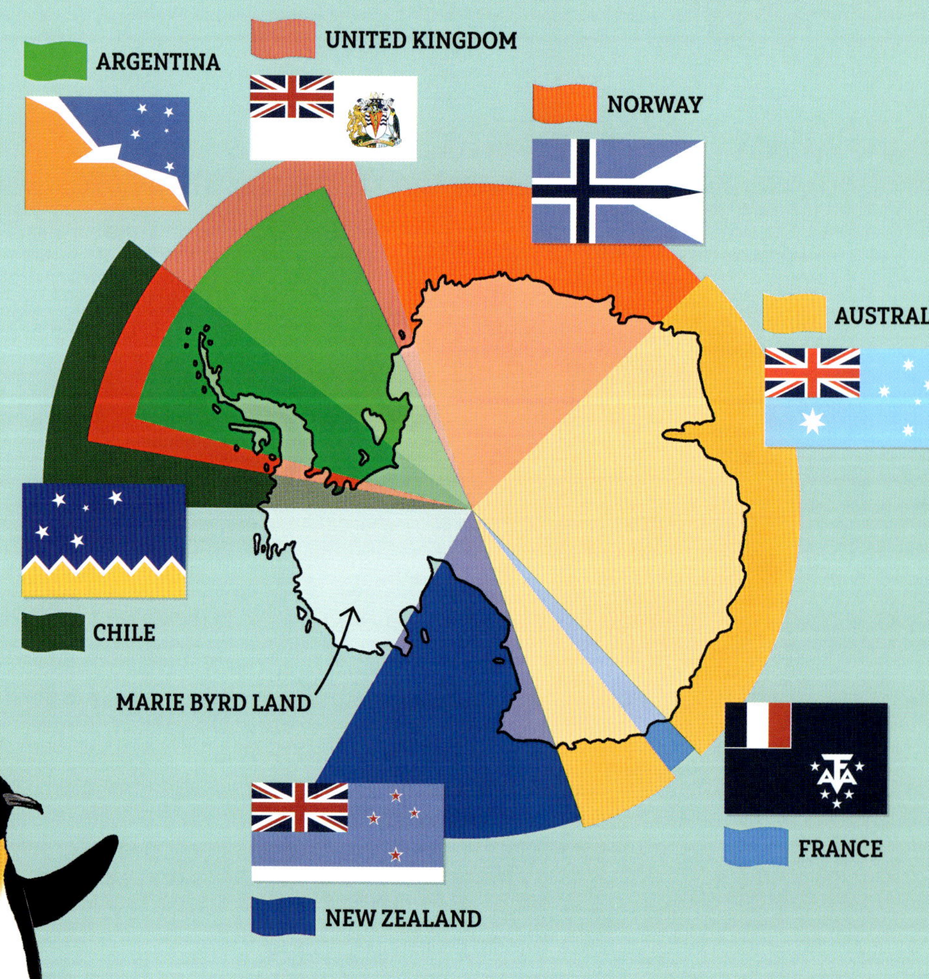

No countries have claimed a large area of Antarctica called Marie Byrd Land. Covering around 0.6 million sq mi (1.6 million sq km), it's the largest unclaimed territory on Earth and is larger than most countries.

OVERSEAS FLAGS

Here's a selection of flags from areas that belong to other countries. Use the page references to spot them on the maps throughout the book.

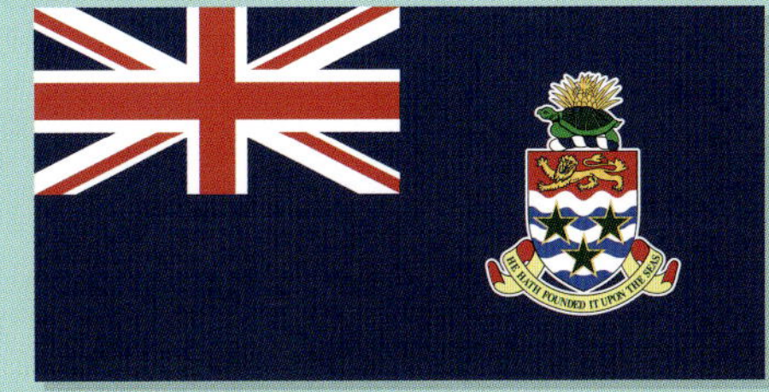

UK—CAYMAN ISLANDS
(see p.15)

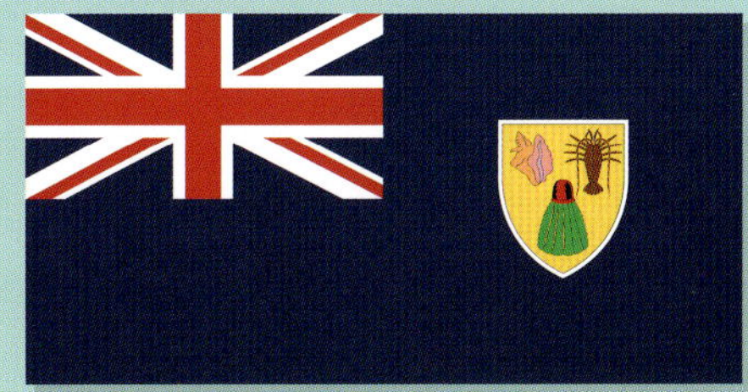

UK—TURKS AND CAICOS ISLANDS
(see p.15)

UK—BRITISH VIRGIN ISLANDS
(see p.15)

UK—ANGUILLA
(see p.15)

UK—MONTSERRAT
(see p.15)

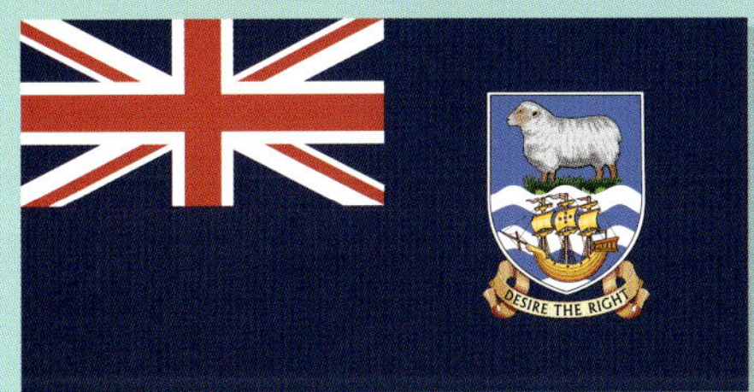

UK—FALKLAND ISLANDS
(see p.25)

UK—SOUTH GEORGIA AND THE SOUTH SANDWICH ISLANDS (see p.25)

UK—GIBRALTAR (see p.33). It's the only British overseas flag not to feature the Union Jack.

UK—PITCAIRN ISLANDS
(see p.85)

USA—PUERTO RICO
(see p.15)

USA—US VIRGIN ISLANDS
(see p.15)

USA—GUAM
(see p.84)

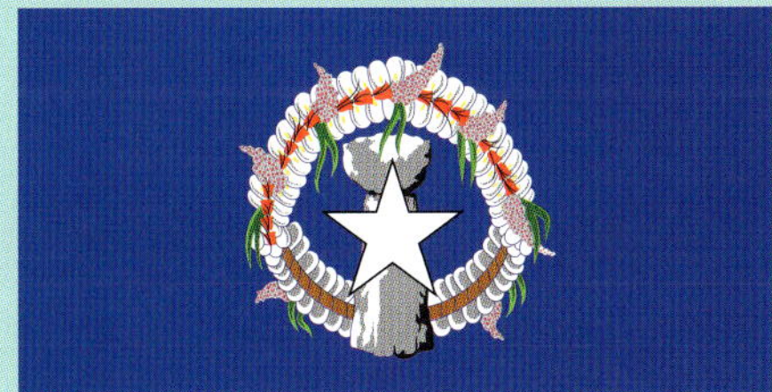

USA—NORTHERN MARIANA ISLANDS
(see p.84)

USA—AMERICAN SAMOA
(see p.85)

NETHERLANDS—ARUBA
(see p.15)

NETHERLANDS—CURAÇAO
(see p.15)

NETHERLANDS—BONAIRE
(see p.15)

NETHERLANDS—ST. MAARTEN
(see p.15)

NETHERLANDS—ST. EUSTATIUS
(see p.15)

FRANCE—ST. MARTIN
(see p.15)

FRANCE—NEW CALEDONIA
(see p.84)

FRANCE—WALLIS AND FUTUNA
(see p.84)

FRANCE—FRENCH POLYNESIA
(see p.85)

For more flags of French overseas territories, see p.41.

DENMARK—GREENLAND
(see p.15)

DENMARK—FAROE ISLANDS
(see p.33)

SPAIN—CANARY ISLANDS
(see p.51)

PORTUGAL—MADEIRA
(see p.51)

AUSTRALIA—COCOS (KEELING) ISLAND (see p.84)

AUSTRALIA—CHRISTMAS ISLAND
(see p.84)

AUSTRALIA—NORFOLK ISLAND
(see p.84)

NEW ZEALAND—COOK ISLANDS
(see p.85)

NEW ZEALAND—TOKELAU
(see p.85)

NEW ZEALAND—NIUE
(see p.84)

CHILE—RAPA NUI (EASTER ISLAND) (see p.85)

GLOSSARY

CANTON A rectangular section in the top left-hand corner of a flag that has a different design than the rest of the flag.

CHARGE A symbol on the field of a flag, such as the maple leaf on the flag of Canada.

CHEVRON A triangle shape on a flag, usually shown coming in from the hoist (left) side.

COAT OF ARMS The official emblem of a country or other institution, usually consisting of a shield shape decorated with symbols.

COLONIAL Relating to a colony—an area of land that is taken over by another country to become part of its empire.

COMMUNIST A type of political system where most of a country's land, buildings, and businesses are owned by the government, not the people. In communist countries, the people don't vote for their leaders.

DEMOCRATIC Relating to democracy, a type of political system in which the people have a say in how their government is run, and choose their leaders by voting.

FESSE A horizontal band (usually of a single color) on a flag design.

FIELD The background color or pattern of a flag.

FIMBRIATION A narrow border usually used to separate two larger areas of color on a flag.

FLAG OF CONVENIENCE A flag of a particular country flown by a ship, not because the ship is from that country, but because it is registered there and pays less tax than it would in its actual country of origin.

FLY The half of the flag farthest from the flagpole; also sometimes used to describe the horizontal length of a flag.

HALYARD A rope attached to the edge of a flag, used for raising and lowering it on a flagpole.

HOIST The half of the flag nearest to the flagpole.

INDIGENOUS Originating in a particular place; Indigenous Peoples are ones who inhabited an area first.

MOTTO A short phrase that has been chosen to represent an institution, such as a country.

NATIONAL FLAG The official flag of a country that is flown by its government and recognized as representing that country across the world.

NORDIC CROSS A design that appears on several Scandinavian flags featuring a cross slightly offset to the left.

OVERSEAS TERRITORY An area that is not a country in its own right but belongs to another country, which may be a great distance away.

PALE A vertical band of color on a flag's design.

PAN-AFRICAN COLORS The colors of red, yellow, and green (and sometimes black) that feature on several African flags to signify African unity and freedom from colonialism.

PAN-ARAB COLORS The colors of black, red, white, and green often used on flags of Arabic-speaking countries of the Middle East and North Africa to signify the unity of the Arab peoples.

PAN-SLAVIC COLORS The colors of red, white, and blue, inspired by the Russian flag, that feature on several countries' flags in Eastern Europe, signifying unity between peoples who speak Slavic languages.

PENNANT A flag that tapers to a point at one end, and is often long and thin.

SOUTHERN CROSS A constellation visible in the Southern Hemisphere that features on several flags in Oceania, usually depicted as being made up of four large stars (as on the flag of New Zealand) or four large stars and one small one (as on the flag of Samoa).

SOVIET UNION A communist state of 15 countries that existed from 1922–91.

TRICOLOR A flag made up of three vertical colored bands (or pales), as in the flag of France, known as the Tricolore.

INDEX